THE GREAT TRAIN HEIST

THE GREAT TRAIN HEIST

The California SMART Taxpayer Rip-off

What Every Voter Should Know About the Upcoming SMART Sales Tax Measure

MICHAEL J. COFFINO

Skyhorse Publishing

Skyhorse Publishing books may be purchased in bulk at special discounts for sales promotion, corporate gifts, fund-raising, or educational purposes. Special editions can also be created to specifications. For details, contact the Special Sales Department, Skyhorse Publishing, 307 West 36th Street, 11th Floor, New York, NY 10018 or info@skyhorsepublishing.com.

Skyhorse® and Skyhorse Publishing® are registered trademarks of Skyhorse Publishing, Inc.®, a Delaware corporation.

Visit our website at www.skyhorsepublishing.com.

10 9 8 7 6 5 4 3 2 1

Library of Congress Cataloging-in-Publication Data is available on file.

Cover design by David Ter-Avanesyan

ISBN: 978-1-5107-8629-5
Ebook ISBN: 978-1-5107-8638-7

Printed in the United States of America

Contents

Introduction

Why Do We Bother? An Introductory Statement from the Gallaher Family

Why did we decide to have a book written about the Sonoma–Marin Area Rail Transit ("SMART")? Why did our family publicly oppose Measure I in 2020, a tax measure put before the Marin and Sonoma taxpayers to further subsidize SMART's expansion and operation? Why do we care?

In the beginning, while we believed that finite tax dollars were better spent elsewhere, our main concern was the lack of transparency and accountability, the persistent failure of SMART to come clean with the public about its problems, including its operating expenses, ridership numbers, user fees, and taxpayer subsidies. We thought the public—those being asked to pay for the rail line operation—deserved to know how much it cost, who it is serving, how it is performing, and the degree to which it has delivered on its promises to voters about the purported public benefits of the transportation program.

Although it didn't take much digging to find answers to these and related questions, it was disturbing to us that this information had not been widely available to the public. We knew that many in the public sector held different opinions about SMART's potential value to local taxpayers, but without disclosed facts, how could taxpayers make an informed decision? It is unfortunate it took a private party with financial resources to do the research and mount the public campaign to make those facts available.

As the research progressed, we saw that many in the affected local communities, especially those instrumental in creating and administering SMART, believe fervently in its mission and, in theory at least, the public good it might bring. This zealous belief in the "rightness" of the cause may explain in part why the public received a distorted and partial accounting of SMART and its operation, why public scrutiny was evaded.

This book furthers and expands on our initial goal: transparency. We wanted to uncover the history of how SMART came to be, how it is funded, what its ridership is, the cost to taxpayers per ride, its impact on traffic congestion and carbon emissions, and so on. In the years that followed Measure I's defeat in 2020, more data became available, bringing a heightened awareness about the rail program. Because we neither have the time nor skills to write a book of this magnitude, we hired a professional writer to shine a light on the SMART story from conception to current operation, a story we believe the public deserves to hear.

We are a Sonoma County family with a multigenerational history and deep roots in the community. We are saddened by the many pressing local needs that exist, which residents are acutely aware of, and believe public funds can be better spent in various, more urgent ways, with far more positive impact benefiting far more people than a project like SMART. We have a homelessness and a housing crisis. We have mental health facility needs. We have roads that need repair. We need rehabilitation centers for both men and women. This is only a partial list. Some may disagree with us and choose funding SMART as a priority. That is their right. But we feel it is imperative that the public make informed decisions regarding SMART.

The Gallaher Family had nothing concrete to gain from its campaign against Measure I, nor in writing this book. Quite the contrary. We have been vilified by local and state politicians and are winning no local popularity contests with local officials or the press. Nor will this effort help our businesses (building and banking) in any way.

We bothered because there are hundreds of millions of taxpayer dollars at stake, and we feel strongly those dollars can and should be better spent elsewhere. At one level, SMART is a complicated story, heavily laden with historical data and information. It is difficult to distill into a simplified rendering. But we believe Mr. Coffino has managed to do just that.

We hope this work brings clarity to the public domain and provides voters the information they need to vote the way they want.

Prologue

Be Careful What You Ask For

It began as a harmless text message, a modest fundraising request for an upcoming political campaign, the kind so routine it almost never raises an eyebrow. This one, however, unwittingly set in motion an incendiary sequence that redefined the public discourse about the controversial Northern California rail line known as the SMART train.

In the summer of 2019, Debora Fudge, chairperson of the Sonoma Marin Area Rail Transit (SMART) board of directors, was making fundraising rounds. Her charge as board member was to drum up dollars for a voter poll and proposed ballot measure to extend an existing period for a sales tax that Sonoma and Marin County taxpayers had approved in 2008.

The 2008 ballot followed four consecutive failed attempts over two decades to convince taxpayers to bankroll a local commuter train. Its terms included a sunset date of 2029, meaning at the time of the 2019 fundraising efforts, a full decade remained on local tax collection. Nonetheless, SMART advocates wanted to extend the taxation period an additional thirty years—all the way to 2059.

As part of her efforts to hit up potential contributors, on June 26, Fudge reached out to Komron Shahhosseini, an advisor to Bill Gallaher, CEO of the Gallaher Companies, a Sonoma County–based developer. As a lifelong, registered Democrat with a deep history of community involvement, Gallaher was a natural target. Fudge stressed to Shahhosseini via text the positive financial impact that a successful commuter rail system might have on developers like Gallaher.

When Shahhosseini did not respond right away, Fudge followed up to emphasize fundraising goals and note that other local developers had shown a willingness to contribute.

Shahhosseini called Fudge. He explained that to proceed further, he needed underlying financial material; that before contributing to the campaign, he had to undertake some diligence to assure project worthiness.

Upon receiving financial documents in response, Shahhosseini noted immediately that the materials lacked detailed ridership data. That struck him as peculiar. Ridership data is a critical benchmark for measuring the financial viability of the rail system and what he'd expect SMART to tout in any effort to raise financial support.

He responded: "Please send or tell me where I can find in-depth ridership numbers. Thanks!"

The subsequent numbers he received exposed a stark disparity between fare revenue and operating costs, meaning a substantial public subsidy per ride. Shahhosseini determined that SMART was generating only $5.47 per ride against operating costs of $60.27 per ride. In other words, based on the figures provided, he concluded that taxpayers were subsidizing

92 percent of the SMART commuter rail system. Surprised, he reverted to Fudge: "That couldn't be right, please tell me where my math is wrong."

While Fudge offered clarifications regarding fare variations and discounted passes, so far as the Shahhosseini could tell, the explanations did not change the basic math that showed an enormous public subsidy, leaving a glaring and problematic financial gap. He told Fudge he didn't want to be difficult, but explained that before devoting funds to the project, "it would be pretty irresponsible doing so without understanding."

From the perspective of the Gallahers, the solicitation process highlighted a tension between supporting the transportation system for a broader community and its touted environmental benefits and the absence of financial fundamentals needed to justify committing funds. Fudge promised to follow up with further financial planning documents upon completion of an expenditure plan and an oversight review. The Gallahers never heard back.

The invitation to participate in the SMART project stoked the curiosity of the Gallaher group, including Molly Flater, daughter of Bill Gallaher. As she took a further look into the situation, with which she had been relatively unfamiliar, she became concerned that SMART may have squandered precious public funds. To make matters worse from the public interest vantage point, she found it troubling that SMART was considering asking taxpayers to absorb an additional $2 billion with the proposed extension.

When Shahhosseini and Flater took a deeper dive into the history of SMART, their initial concerns heightened, including that:

1. SMART may not only be performing well below reasonable expectations but may be the worst-performing train system in the nation.
2. SMART did not seem to be serving the low-income community, but rather residents earning six figures a year.
3. SMART seemed far from the "green" project proponents portrayed. On the contrary, the SMART train seemed destined to generate a net negative environmental impact.

Worse, it appeared to Flater that the pro-SMART campaign rested precariously on a collection of falsehoods; taxpayers may have been sold a bill of goods. If so, she reasoned, didn't taxpayers deserve more accurate information so they could make an informed decision, should the SMART board move forward with the new tax measure?

It was possible that the financial information the SMART CFO was compiling could cast things in a different light or explain things better. But for whatever reason, those materials never came, and as time went on, it became increasingly clear that SMART deemed the Gallahers a lost fundraising cause. Whatever the explanation, neither Fudge nor the SMART CFO contacted Shahhosseini again.

***

In the fall of 2019, SMART commissioned a voter poll about the proposed tax extension. The results showed that three out of four voters would likely approve a ballot measure that extended the existing sales tax until 2059. The poll tally evidently persuaded the SMART board to proceed with the ballot measure (Measure I) at the upcoming primary election in March 2020.

Concerned about the direction of the SMART project and the potential new money grab from taxpayers, Flater commissioned her own poll. It showed the opposite of the SMART poll—that "informed" voters would turn away the attempted increase in taxes when told the facts of the full cost of the ballot measure and of SMART's performance—but also that any ballot measure would likely muster less than 55 percent support, well below the two-thirds legal requirement.

The two polls were ships passing in the night, one potentially advancing a false positive, the other potentially a false negative.

Based on the poll results and preliminary research, Flater felt a rising moral obligation to mount an educational campaign to inform voters. From what she had seen, when scrutinized, SMART was nothing like the image it projected to the public. She felt local leaders had effectively hoodwinked the public, and from a social policy and public service standpoint, the SMART train was a looming disaster.

In early January 2020, as the March 3 election fast approached, Flater, working with the NotSoSmart organization, a local nonprofit group formed to oppose the train initiative, went live with an opposition campaign using radio ads, flyers, and a website. The essential points were:

- SMART had hidden its ridership numbers from the general public, and when pressured to disclose, misstated them by a magnitude of 100,000.
- Each SMART trip cost taxpayers $100 a ride.
- SMART added, not reduced, greenhouse gas emissions.[1]
- The proposed ballot would provide SMART an additional $2.4 billion over the proposed taxation period, which would hit working families, who were not the benefactors of the rail system, the hardest.

- In sum, Measure I cost so much in exchange for so little—and without adequate transparency and budget oversight.

They further questioned the prudence of asking taxpayers to shell out billions of more dollars when SMART's annual operating expenses had exceeded twice what SMART had projected when petitioning for the sales tax in 2008.[2] They also reminded the public that, according to the *Santa Rosa Press Democrat*—with its staunch pro-SMART editorial board—SMART trains on average rode more than 80 percent empty[3]; that, according to the *Marin Independent Journal*—which urged that voters reject Measure I—serious inefficiencies existed in the SMART operation, including a failure to connect with other public transit systems; and that SMART had refused to implement several civil grand jury recommendations designed to improve the agency's financial oversight and communication with the public (more on that later).[4]

The opposition braced for SMART proponents to engage them in a productive debate on these many substantive issues. That, however, is not what happened.

On January 15, 2020, the California Fair Political Practices Commission (FPPC) informed Flater that Sonoma resident Dani Sheehan-Meyer had filed a complaint against her, an administrative action that triggers the potential of criminal penalties in the form of a misdemeanor and monetary fines.[5] The complaint, according to the FPPC, did not quarrel with the factual content of the campaign materials. Rather, Sheehan-Meyer alleged that Flater had failed to file certain requisite form documents with the commission, an alleged failure to properly disclose her funding role. Sheehan-Meyer went further, enlisting a string of personal comments unrelated to the SMART campaign itself, including that "Molly Flater is the daughter of multi-millionaire developer Bill Gallaher," that the Gallaher family at one time created the "largest PAC in Sonoma County" in support of local political candidates, and that the Gallahers allegedly "had funneled money illegally" into a political campaign years ago.

In response, counsel for the NotSoSmart committee, the direct benefactor of Ms. Flater's anti–Measure I financial support, dismantled the FPPC complaint, showing that it had the facts wrong and the NotSoSmart committee (and Flater) had complied both with the letter and spirit of applicable legal requirements. In response, the FPPC closed the file, taking no enforcement action.

The FPPC complaint, however, lacking in merit as it was, raised a separate and disturbing issue. It appeared that the hastily drawn complaint—patched together little more than twenty-four hours after the launch of the anti–Measure I campaign—represented not a concerned citizen's well-intentioned effort to assure campaign law compliance, but rather SMART's use of a shill to repress an opposition voice: Sheeran-Meyer was the Treasurer of the Stay Green Keep SMART campaign.

Subsequent events showed more of the same.

On January 17, 2020, two days after the filing of the FPPC complaint, Jared Huffman, a Democrat member of the US House of Representatives serving California's 2nd congressional district (now covering the counties of Marin, Sonoma, Mendocino, Trinity, Humboldt, and Del Norte) posted this on Facebook:

> Right out of the Koch/Adelson/Citizens United playbook, a conservative developer is spending over $500k to defeat the quarter cent sales tax needed to keep operating and building out the SMART rail and trail transit system. Killing SMART makes no sense whatsoever we've spent over 650M

> building a system we've attracted tens of millions in federal and state grants, and there's more to come. We just opened Larkspur and downtown Novato stations, we're opening Windsor station next year and we'll get to Healdsburg/ Cloverdale soon thereafter. But a mega-rich developer who likes sprawl and hates the train and the transit-oriented development and open space protection it encourages, says "kill it." With the 2/3 vote requirement to pass Measure I in March we're now going to have a tough, expressive campaign. Please, for the sake of this community and our future planning, transportation and environmental needs, vote YES on Measure I . . . spread the word about this dark money stunt . . . and stay tuned for how you can help.

The Huffman attack was peculiar for a number of reasons.

For starters, the existence of the train would advantage the Gallaher group as a developer. It could potentially increase population density and, by law, provide expedited approval processes for residential developments near SMART stations. If anything, opposing the train was against their financial interests.

Another oddity was the attempt of Representative Huffman to associate Bill Gallaher—a registered Democrat with a long record of community contributions, including efforts to help the adoption of foreign-born children, a major donor to local Boys and Girls clubs, the largest donor to the Redwood Empire Food Bank, and the 2013 winner of the "Leadership Institute in Sustainability" Award by the Leadership Institute for Ecology and Economy—with the likes of the infamous Koch brothers or Republican megadonor and casino owner Sheldon Adelson, who flooded American politics with dark money in the wake of the infamous Supreme Court decision in the Citizens United case.

Equally mystifying was the sneering reference to "dark money." The dismissal of the bogus FPPC complaint proved that the funding was the precise opposite of "dark money" and, it is worth noting, SMART thought the Gallaher money green enough when it wanted some several months earlier.

What's more, late February media reports pegged financial support for the "no" campaign at about $1.7 million and the "yes" campaign over $1.2 million, a delta that hardly justified social media histrionics about a money "stunt."[6] Facts, they do matter.

Content to smear with insinuation, Representative Huffman sidestepped any attempt to refute the factual statements in the opposition campaign. And he left unexplained why SMART, in 2020, with ten years left on its taxation period, "needed" $2 billion in new tax revenues to keep the train "operating and building out," especially since, according to him, "we've attracted tens of millions in federal and state grants, and there is more to come."

The attacks continued.

On February 5, 2020, with the election less than a month away, the pro-SMART contingent distributed a flyer directly attacking the Gallaher family. The banner read: "The Gallaher Family is Trying to Commit Train Robbery—By Taking SMART Away From Us." Beneath the banner was a man standing next to a train thrusting a gun in the faces of train engine personnel, their hands thrust into the air in obeisance to the armed robbers, which included two other men menacingly holding rifles. The adjoining text included this: "WHILE THE GALLAHER FAMILY FLIES AROUND IN THEIR PRIVATE JET, THEY ARE TRYING TO DEPRIVE THE WORKING PEOPLE OF THE NORTH BAY—TEACHERS, NURSES, STUDENTS—OF A GREEN ALTERNATIVE TO SITTING IN TRAFFIC ON HIGHWAY 101 . . . DON'T LET

THE GALLAHER CLAN GET AWAY WITH STEALING IT FROM US."

Was the parade of individual attacks business as usual, the kind of corrosive mentality that had slid onto the national stage in modern times as the new norm, a page plucked from the cynical, mean-spirited political playbook? Or were they something else entirely, something more strategic, a purposeful way to shield the public eye from taking too close a look? Did the pro-SMART contingent fear an open, rational public debate that centered on facts and scientific data, content to find sanctuary in ad hominem attacks? And if so, how would the public react to the two divergent approaches for debating the important issues on the table? Would character assassination win the day over substantive dialogue, or vice versa?

***

Voters answered on March 3, 2020. Measure I garnered only 49.8 percent in Sonoma County and 53.5 percent in Marin County support among voting taxpayers,[7] precisely what the Flater commissioned poll had projected, and well below the two-thirds approval required for a special tax initiative. For the fifth time in six tries, voters rejected the sales tax agenda.

But perhaps more importantly, voters affirmed that the bar for public discussion about the bona fides of the SMART project had elevated. No longer could proponents presume knee-jerk voter acquiescence and blind adherence to "trust us" or rely upon inebriating bromides like "green" or take refuge in personal attacks on those offering contrary or critical views. Facts, accountability, and transparency each had taken up places at the table.

WHILE THE GALLAHER FAMILY FLIES HIGH IN THEIR JET –
THEY WANT US TO SIT IN TRAFFIC DOWN BELOW
Sonoma County tycoon Bill Gallaher and his family fly around in their private jet, so traffic isn't a problem for them.
For the rest of us – we are sitting in traffic on Highway 101 or taking the SMART train.
The family of tycoon Bill Gallaher has spent $849,000 to defeat Measure I, threatening to take the SMART train off the tracks and kill the green alternative to Highway 101 traffic.
THE GALLAHERS' ANTI-GREEN RECORD
The Gallaher family is building quite an anti-green record, opposing SMART's green alternative to Highway 101, flying on their private jet and suing to prevent Sonoma County cities from taking actions to fight climate change.
Don't let the Gallaher clan get away with it. When you read the misinformation they are spreading, be sure to go to StayGreenKeepSMART.org to get all the facts.
YES ON I
Stay Green, Keep SMART
BY MAIL OR ON MARCH 3:
STAY GREEN, KEEP SMART
YES ON MEASURE I

The June 2023 Marin County Civil Grand Jury Report, in reviewing the results of Measure I, stated: "As the March 2020 election results made clear, voters did not believe SMART's Board and existing management had accomplished what they promised, nor did voters have confidence and trust in the Board's performance."[8]

The increased public attention brought into clearer focus the history of SMART and its long-term viability. There was much the public did not know. People on both sides of the equation can and should debate the facts and data and be encouraged to take divergent positions on policy. Decisions at the voter level about taxation and how to use public funds can only occur effectively with an airing of all relevant facts.

1

Best-Laid Plans?

The SMART train has roots, however tenuous, in local rail history, sprung from the pursuit of ideas to address urban and suburban transportation challenges in the modern era.

California has a storied railroad history dating to 1869, when the first US transcontinental railroad connected the recently admitted state to the rest of the union.[9] Its history includes a robust period of passenger rail service in the early part of the twentieth century in Northern California courtesy of the Northern Pacific Railroad.[10] And while eventually use of rail for passenger transport in California and throughout the United States suffered a major decline with the expansive development of roads and the proliferation of cars, modern-day advancements ushered in new urban systems such as, in Northern California, the San Francisco Bay Area Rapid Transit (BART), primarily serving movement from Bay Area suburbs to San Francisco, and the San Francisco Municipal Railway (Muni), serving intracity transit needs.

But despite those transportation upgrades, Northern California rail systems continued their steady decline. By the early 1980s, freight rail lines in Northern California were in dire straits, with a wide range of vested interests—e.g., government officials, railroad owners, politicians, and environmentalists—in a tussle about what to do with a ruinous rail line of track that spanned from Marin County to Eureka.[11] While a remote stretch that hugged the banks of the Eel River, connecting Humboldt County with points south, was the worst of the lot,[12] it was generally acknowledged that the entire rail track offered little reason for optimism.[13] And, for all intents and purposes, a single track that ran from Marin County northward through Sonoma County became effectively abandoned.[14]

Rail advocates—believers in rail as the transportation future—seized the opportunity to try and secure a railroad right-of-way to create a commuter line to run north of San Francisco, specifically between the bordering counties of Marin and Sonoma.[15] Other interests converged, including those intent on maintaining the existing line for freight purposes—a separate and complex story that would rear its head down the road—and others who saw a window to inveigle politicians and community influencers into including a lengthy scenic trail to run parallel with any secured commuter line. The unfolding vision depicted a commuter rail line primarily to transport locals to and from work on a regular basis, leaving cars in the garage, reducing traffic congestion, and producing a net positive impact on air quality.

A local commuter rail system that carried passengers *within* suburbs and rural locations, in contrast to a system that connected suburban and rural residents to sprawling business-infused urban centers like New York, lacked a successful historical model, other than what existed about one hundred years ago during the pre–motor vehicle era. Indeed, when a Santa Rosa Chamber of Commerce member visited

Portland to gain insight into how its intra-suburban commuter rail system had fared, he was told in no uncertain terms not to do it. The odds, it seemed, were painfully long.

Still, the notion of a local commuter rail system held the potential of emotional appeal for taxpayers committed to changing the environment and quality of life. It fit nicely within the core cultures of Marin and Sonoma, the kind of project for which community leaders could entice local taxpayers to foot the bill. Everyone wants reduced traffic and better air quality, the thinking went. Why not tee up a sales tax measure for voter approval?

In July 1990, the Marin County Board of Supervisors put Measure A on the upcoming November ballot, asking taxpayers to authorize an increase of one cent in their sales tax obligations to fund a light rail system between Larkspur and Novato. The next month, the Sonoma County Board of Supervisors followed suit, asking its resident taxpayers to absorb an increase in their sales taxes by one-half of 1 percent, a portion of which was for the commuter rail line.

The measures got classified as "general" tax initiatives on the basis they were subject to the discretion of a general-purpose government, meaning the counties could use the collected funds as they saw fit.[16] A proposed general tax required only a simple majority voter approval.[17]

In contrast, "special taxes" were those earmarked to benefit a specific district or constituency and limited the way in which the governmental entity could spend the funds, effectively tying its hands to a specific purpose. They required a supermajority of two-thirds, a requirement rooted in California's famous 1978 Proposition 13, which amended the California Constitution to establish a base year value for property tax assessments, limit the tax rate and assessment increases for real property, and raise the voter approval levels for imposition of certain taxes.[18]

The general tax classification of the two measures, each seeking to impose a tax for local commuter projects, was dubious, but in the end academic. The Marin County measure received a 40.3 percent favorable vote and the Sonoma County version 46.1 percent, both failing.

If at First?

Several years later, in November 1998, undeterred by the first taxpayer rejection, rail advocates rolled the dice again. This time they asked taxpayers of Marin (Measure B) and Sonoma (Measure C) to shell out their hard-earned money by approving an additional half-cent sales tax to help build a light rail commuter system, levied over a twenty-year period, seeking to raise $300 million and $627 million, respectively. The ballot measures also proposed to add lanes to Highway 101 and bike trails, among other improvements, as well as preserve thousands of acres of open space.[19]

The underlying thinking had not changed, that an intra-suburban commuter line was essential to deflating bloated traffic conditions on Highway 101, a troubling local circumstance that advocates urged would worsen as new residents (and thus workers) continued to flock in droves to Marin and Sonoma Counties.

US House Representative Lynn Woolsey (D-San Rafael), serving a district that covered all of Marin and some of Sonoma, distilled the proponent point of view this way:

> I think what the two counties are doing is very important for the future. Congestion on the highway is holding up commuters and families in both counties. This will give people a reason to get out of their cars.[20]

As will be seen, Representative Woolsey's comments drew on unsustainable assumptions about the nexus between the proposed commuter transit system and traffic congestion. For the time being, however, the crux of her comments became a rallying cry, a call to action to mitigate horrific local traffic congestion, a banner proponents have waved persistently to this day.[21]

The rationale was (and is) that the two neighboring counties, particularly Sonoma, would have massive residential development clustered near proposed train stations, providing residents easy and environmentally superior access to employment locations in and between the two counties.[22]

Detractors argued, based on projected demographics, residential development patterns, and work locations, that the system would never enjoy enough riders to make it worthwhile, the costs would be astronomical, and that, regardless, the system would have no meaningful impact on Highway 101 traffic. They argued that proponents had fallen victim to a massive pipe dream, some dubbing the proposed rail system a "one-way railroad to nowhere."

Time would tell which of the two groups earned "I told you so" bragging rights.

Accompanying the 1998 measures were Measure A in Marin and Measure B in Sonoma, which sought to allocate the money to upgrade existing tracks (once used by the Northwestern Pacific Railroad), build and upgrade rail stations, and purchase diesel-powered light-rail cars. Rail service would connect rural Cloverdale in Sonoma with San Rafael (the Marin County seat).

Voters once again said no. While 63.3 percent approved the plan, only 42.5 percent approved the tax increase to fund it.

Third Time the Charm?

In 2000, Sonoma County decided to go it alone, putting a largely recycled measure on its ballot (Measure C) for local taxpayer consideration. Measure C sought to impose on county taxpayers a sales tax increase for sixteen years—raising an estimated $348 million—to build a local commuter rail service between Cloverdale and the Sonoma-Marin boundary line. In other words, Sonoma limited its new vision to *intra-county* transportation, leaving workers who lived in Sonoma and worked in Marin out to dry. Sonoma also promised to spend some of the tax bounty to improve bus service, build bicycle paths, and make other infrastructure improvements.

One problem with Measure C—apart from its abandonment of a regional solution in concert with Marin County—was that it would only raise about half the funds the proposed project admitted it needed. The proponents presumed—and asked taxpayers to bank on the presumption—that if taxpayers shelled out the dollars, the projects would qualify for matching federal and state grants.

The Sonoma County Conservation Action, a nonprofit organization in Santa Rosa that styles itself a "nonpartisan, political arm of Sonoma County's environmental movement," branded Measure C a political ploy for its snubbing of cooperation with Marin County.[23]

Because Measure C sought to impose a special tax for transportation, its passage required a two-thirds majority. The "Yes" votes totaled 60.3 percent and the measure failed.

Local taxpayers in Marin and Sonoma had now rejected a tax measure to finance a commuter rail system three times in a single decade, a track record that fairly raised the question: Was it time to respect the will of the people?

A Phoenix Rising?

Apparently not. Rail advocates refused to hoist a white flag. Spurned at the ballot box, they turned to state power brokers to help launch their ambitious project. They sought to create a political infrastructure—a special legislative district—that, once established, would command funding if only because it existed and needed money to operate. To advance the cause, California Assemblyman Joe Nation (D-San Rafael) stepped up to the plate.

To give Assemblyman Nation traction, the Sonoma County Transportation Authority and the Marin County Congestion Management Agency (later the Transportation Authority of Marin) retained a consultant to conduct a study, funded by the California Department of Transportation (Caltrans). The study would explore multimodal transportation alternatives in Sonoma and Marin Counties with an eye toward reducing traffic congestion on Highway 101. The mission of the study sought to determine "how to *most efficiently spend public money* on transportation improvements and how to create a pattern of land use that can most efficiently take best advantage of transportation options while maintaining a high quality of life for Sonoma and Marin County residents" (emphasis added).

The considered scenarios included adding more HOV lanes and completing an existing HOV lane (through San Rafael), reconfiguring freeway exchanges, introducing commuter rail service, improving existing bus transit system, and enhancing bicycle and pedestrian modes of movement. Despite the in-depth analysis, the study concluded, among many other things, that there was "no silver bullet" and that "no scenario will substantially change fundamental travel behavior . . . because the increment of growth between 1995 and

2015 is not large enough to change the fundamental character of the North Bay; also people in the future will most likely have a strong propensity to drive."[24]

The study settled on a hodgepodge approach, betting that various approaches operating separately with harmonious goals would bring about the needed impact on traffic congestion in tandem. Oddly, other than passing references, the study did not seriously consider paid-for express lanes or congestion pricing, two national models that have gained significant traction for effectively battling traffic.

The study recommended, among other things, formation of a commission to help design a passenger train service for the two counties. The commission, comprised of two supervisors and three city council members from each county, after an eighteen-month process, voted in favor of forming a new commuter rail transit agency to run sixty-eight miles from Cloverdale to San Rafael, with eleven stations on the route. As funding for the commuter line, they contemplated primarily a one-cent sales tax imposed on Sonoma and Marin taxpayers and rail bond funds from the 1990 Clean Air and Transportation Improvement Act (CATIA). The commission did not recommend use of congestion pricing as an alternative.

In response, Assemblyman Nation authored Assembly Bill 2224 (2004) to, among other things, create an administrative "district" as the governing body for the commuter rail system. On August 12, 2002, the California Assembly voted in favor of AB 2224, 49–22 and the Senate 22–14, which Governor Gray Davis signed into law on August 31.

AB 2224 amended sections 53090 of the California Government Code and 20216 of the Public Contract Code, and, most importantly, added Part 16 to Division 10 the Public Utilities Code ("PUC"), commencing with section 105000.

Section 105001 of the PUC sets forth the purpose of the new legislation:

> It is the intent of the Legislature in enacting this part to provide for a unified, comprehensive institutional structure for the ownership and governance of a passenger rail system within the Counties of Sonoma and Marin that shall operate in harmony with existing freight service that operates upon the same rail line and serves the Counties of Humboldt, Marin, Mendocino, Napa, and Sonoma. It is the further intent of the Legislature that the district established by this act may succeed to the powers, duties, obligations, liabilities, immunities, and exemptions of both the Sonoma-Marin Area Rail Transit Commission and the Northwestern Pacific Railroad Authority upon their dissolution. Because there is no general law under which this district could be formed, the adoption of a special act and the formation of a special district is required.[25]

Accordingly, the statute created the "Sonoma-Marin Rail Transit District" (the "SMART District") coterminous with the boundaries of Marin and Sonoma counties. The new law granted the SMART District permission to provide a rail transit system for the transportation of passengers and their incidental baggage.

In a nutshell, the legislation allowed the SMART District to build and operate a seventy-mile passenger train and multiuse pathway from Cloverdale in Sonoma to Larkspur in Marin.

The legislation directed that any rates and charges the board levied for rail transit service had to be "reasonable," a term the legislature did not define.

The legislature also imposed on the SMART District the duty to "work with the North Coast Railroad Authority, the

Federal Railroad Administration, and any of its successor agencies, to achieve *safe, efficient*, and compatible operations of both passenger rail and freight service along the rail line in Sonoma and Marin Counties."[26]

By virtue of the legislation, the SMART District holds in public trust ownership of seventy miles of railroad right-of-way, a rail corridor that runs parallel to Highway 101, and, according to its website, is "charged with planning, engineering, evaluating and implementing passenger train service and corridor maintenance from Cloverdale to Larkspur."

Here is how SMART describes its mission:

> Traffic congestion along [the Highway 101] corridor has increased dramatically in the last decade and it is now ranked by Caltrans as one of the most congested freeways in the Bay Area. More than 80% of all North Bay commercial, residential and educational facilities are located along the SMART corridor. SMART trains provide a safe, reliable, and efficient transportation alternative to traffic and congestion on Highway 101. In addition, SMART enhances and improves the region's land use policies and preservation of agricultural lands by restricting stations to incorporated areas.[27]

After years of setbacks, SMART advocates had procured a political vehicle to realize their vision of a local commuter rail line that they hoped would make a major dent in traffic congestion and improve the quality of life for Marin and Sonoma residents.

Several burning questions loomed, however, each a variation on a central theme:

Did the SMART train make financial and social policy sense?

If not, would political and community leadership step up?

Would they swallow hard, admit the mistake, and embrace other more effective and reliable means of achieving the laudable goals that spawned the project?

A thunderous ride lay ahead.

2

A Pattern of Ballot Box Failure

How Many Times Do Taxpayers Have to Say No?

California law does not limit how often proponents of the same legislative measure may return to voters for approval after repeated failures. The voting system has nothing comparable to our national pastime's "three strikes and you're out."

But it is reasonable to question the bona fides of repeated attempts over a relatively short period to persuade voters to pay for something they have made clear they do not want to pay for. In most circles, politicians are expected to serve the will of at least the "median" voter, that core constituency whose collective point of view the electoral system favors, and shape legislative initiatives accordingly. But that is a principle that can (and often does) get lost in the shuffle of power, ego, and self-interest. When politicians and their supporters keep returning to the well for the same approval over and over again, it's not as if they don't know what voters don't want. A pattern of consistent election results speaks volumes. Rather, it reasonably can be viewed as a concerted effort to wear down the voting public until proponents get what they want, as if they are saying, "We know what's best for you. Trust us on this one."

In the wake of the several failed ballot attempts that sought to convince taxpayers to subsidize an ambitious local rail project, supporters of SMART commissioned a poll to test the waters yet again, asking whether taxpayers might nonetheless approve a half-cent sales tax. The polling results did not encourage; they were negative, voters in essence saying, "Been there, done that." In response, SMART forces did not retreat. As Bonnie Nelson, a consultant Marin County hired to facilitate the approval process, glibly told the *Marin Independent Journal* in 2004: "This is more like dating than marriage. There is still a chance to change our minds."[28]

SMART considered yet another approach, proposing a quarter-cent tax, a lower threshold of financial hurt that they thought might turn voters around. Would reducing the pain, ever so slightly for the individual pocketbook, increase chances of pay dirt? The problem was that available data suggested a quarter-cent sales tax hike would fall far short of generating funds needed to operate the rail system.[29] Why ask for tax dollars that will not do the job?

But SMART proponents were undeterred. They commissioned a third party (J. Moore Methods) to conduct a public research poll to test voter appetite, the stated goal of which was to "measure the disposition of 'likely General Election voters' towards funding passenger rail through a ¼ cent sales tax measure." It summarized the polling results for the public this way: "Support for a SMART ¼ cent rail tax ranges from 64% to 75%, indicating a very good chance of passage. Estimated mid-point district-wide support for such a measure is at 69.5%."[30]

Presumably emboldened by the poll, they put Measure R on the 2006 ballot, seeking to impose a quarter-cent sales tax on Marin and Sonoma County residents to fund SMART. They pegged the starting date for the tax at April 1, 2007, commencing an annual collection to last twenty years.[31]

After rejection of five similar rail measures combined for the two counties since 1990, Measure R marked the first time taxpayers in both counties would vote as a single block on whether to fund the North Bay rail line. Using a combined measure for both counties was a shrewd strategy to maneuver around the two-thirds approval requirement, specifically to overwhelm the anticipated negative Marin County vote, previously a problem because of having separate county votes, each of which had to comply. Marginalize Marin County and that might do the trick.

As news about a ramp-up to the ballot circulated, the *Marin Independent Journal* (the *Marin IJ*) ran a three-part series on the SMART train. It kicked off the series with a pithy summary of the opposition point of view: "PIE IN THE SKY. Growth inducing. The train to nowhere."[32]

The paper decried the massive price tag, then only $200 million, a cost that SMART officers conceded would likely go higher after "detailed analyses are done." SMART also boasted to the *Marin IJ* that the public supported the measure.[33]

The cornerstone of the SMART endeavor hinged on the assumption that the proposed local railway would displace enough cars on Highway 101 traffic to justify both spending a significant amount of money, primarily local sales tax dollars, and injecting pollutants into the atmosphere from diesel train emissions. If that assumption turned out to be flawed, if the impact on traffic was either slight or nonexistent, the result would be greater pollution and an utter waste of precious public funds.

As with the promise of most major infrastructure projects, pre-implementation studies can vary and conflict, generating a wide range of arguments on either side. Performance over time, however, tends to serve up data to commend or put a lie to the project's working assumptions and often the public must await a record of program operations to know for sure. In the case of SMART, the factual record developed down the road would eventually put the lie to the traffic assumptions, exposing them as initially bold and tantalizing but demonstrably false. The failing would trace to a failure to comprehend how intra-suburban traffic works; the realities of local demographics; the types of drivers using Highway 101; a refusal to consider evolving modern methods for easing traffic congestion effectively; and more recently, the unanticipated proliferation of remote working habits thanks to the COVID pandemic.

For the time being, however, SMART faced its next electoral battle. Measure R proponents argued, first and foremost, contrary to its own studies that concluded the train was not a "silver bullet,"[34] that SMART is an "affordable and convenient alternative" to traffic gridlock on Highway 101 in Marin and Sonoma counties. This, despite the fact that Lillian Hames, SMART's general manager, conceded a year earlier to the *Marin IJ*: "It will not work for every Highway 101 trip, but it will give residents an alternative,"[35]—hardly a ringing endorsement for such a massively expensive and ambitious project. Her comments echoed an earlier similar observation of Farhad Mansourian, then Marin's public works director and later general manager for SMART: "It won't solve everything, but it would be a beginning. We need a lot of help."[36]

SMART touted the added benefit of improving air quality by trading diesel-operating trains for gas-guzzling cars. They highlighted the "relaxed" and reduced trip times between Santa Rosa and San Rafael and Novato, although in doing so failed to account for what is dubbed "the last-mile problem": travel time to and from train stations and to and from ultimate destinations.[37]

Opponents pushed back hard on the traffic argument. They pointed out that SMART's own Environmental Impact Report stated the train would not reduce traffic on Highway 101, drawing on studies that show more than 70 percent of drivers using Highway 101 in both counties drive alone and that most will not switch to a train.[38] They added that SMART's Environmental Impact Report (EIR) estimated only 230 Sonoma County residents would take morning trains to Marin and that the train will not connect with San Francisco, Oakland, and BART.[39] With those key commuter destinations off the map, what is the point, they maintained, echoing the reference in the *Marin IJ* that the train that goes no farther south than San Rafael is "the train to nowhere."

The other nagging issue was money. How much should SMART spend on this project? More to the point, how many local tax dollars should be devoted to the project and to what end? And given all the grave questions about the merits of the rail line, what steps would the SMART board take to demonstrate fiscal responsibility? Indeed, as the *Marin IJ* reported in March 2004, postmortem polling after the failure of the recent sales tax measure "showed that voters didn't trust officials to spend the money as specified in the plan," a fissure that would plague SMART leadership time and again.[40] Proponents said don't worry, we will be fiscally responsible, but did not disclose a detailed financial plan or the overall cost of the project. Their penchant for playing fast and loose with financial data would later become the subject of civil grand jury criticism.

Taking a dive into SMART financials, opponents gleaned that the SMART project was a classic boondoggle, like a holiday toy train set that went around and around, tickling the enthusiasm of a cheering political assemblage but failing to deliver any return to taxpayers. It appeared at the time that the project would cost taxpayers an estimated $1.4 billion over twenty years, a staggering amount of money for the circumstances, and a sum that assumed the project would be completed on budget, almost always wishful thinking. As opponents summed it up, "The train is very expensive, carries few passengers, and doesn't take people where they want to go."[41]

The battle lines were drawn, one side imploring the public to trust them, that they'd deliver a form of public transportation that will change the quality of life for two counties, and the other urging the public not to drink the Kool-Aid, that proponents would fail to deliver on their many promises, that the project was doomed to failure. The late Jan Taber, then with the Environmental Protection Agency in San Francisco, offered this comment about the upcoming sales tax measure: "They always promise things, but will it really help? It never seems to."[42]

Voters, once again, turned SMART advocates away, rejecting Measure R, which required two-thirds approval, with a 65.3 percent combined vote for the two counties (70.1 percent in favor in Sonoma County and 57.5 percent in favor in Marin).[43]

Where did that leave SMART? As a legislatively created special district, they had their backs to the wall. Voters had delivered six legislative defeats to SMART and comparable predecessor rail line initiatives, an extraordinary string of losses. But not surprisingly, given the pattern, familiar defeat did not faze SMART advocates. They were hell-bent on going at it again. While the dust on Measure R's grave was still fresh, they pinned a new measure to the 2008 ballot, this time Measure Q, another combined county initiative, a Measure R rerun, seeking to impose a quarter-cent sales tax on Marin and Sonoma County residents for twenty years.

The voting campaign saw both sides recycle 2006 arguments, with some spins.

Proponents appealed more this time to environmental and lifestyle sensibilities. They entreated voters to approve the measure to "protect the environment, relieve traffic, and provide for our long-term transportation future." They argued that in addition to SMART pulling people out of their cars and off Highway 101 and putting them into train seats, the construction of a companion bicycle-pedestrian path would have a similar impact and thus taxpayers would be funding two new transportation alternatives. They cautioned that a "no" vote would imperil the "local economy and environment" by forcing residents to continue depending on roads and driving, calling Measure Q "a SMART transportation solution."[44]

Opponents kept focusing on the quid pro quo. They stressed the prohibitive costs of a project that would deliver little in return, pointing out that "too few people would take the train to reduce traffic congestion, and trains would stop traffic every 15 minutes during peak periods," and to make matters worse, the trains would leave passengers "high and dry" from ultimate destinations. For example, if commuters wanted to visit San Francisco, the train would leave them "a quarter mile from the [local] ferry terminal." If commuters planned to use the Sonoma County airport when its operations resumed in 2007, they would have to find a second form of transportation from the end of the train line to the airport to make their flights. How is that efficient or sensible, opponents argued? They also reminded the public that, from an environmental perspective, SMART trains would run on diesel and would generate carbon emissions injurious to heart and lungs, increase noise and vibrations, disrupting quiet enjoyment of neighborhoods and damaging real estate values, and destroy approximately thirty acres of wetlands and preserves, critical facts SMART swept under the rug.[45]

To their credit, this time SMART advocates prevailed, obtaining a combined vote of 69.5 percent in the two counties, slightly less than 3 percent over what was needed (73.5 percent approval in Sonoma County and 62.6 percent in Marin County).[46] The strategy of combining the counties into a single voting block did the trick. Otherwise, Measure Q would have failed because the Marin County vote did not produce two-thirds approval. But it raised a troubling question: Was it fair for Marin County taxpayers, who did *not* approve the measure, to subsize the rail program for Sonoma County residents, the primary beneficiaries *of* the measure?

What else explained voter response in 2008 after so many tries?

Many theories circulated. Some deduced it was the coincidence of a spike in gas prices, that voters concerned about paying more for fuel knee-jerked approval for a transit program that promised fewer cars. Some conjectured about the "Obama" factor, that his presidential candidacy brought out otherwise dormant left-leaning voters, tilting the table just enough to get the measure over the top. Others projected that the thin prevailing margin reflected voters tired of the drumbeat of constant requests for their approval and finally succumbed.

Regardless, SMART proponents had turned voters around, getting permission to hit them with more taxes to subsidize the train. While they still faced getting the operation up and running and delivering on the many promises they had made, they had secured bragging rights.

The celebration did not last long.

Two years after approval of Measure Q, the Marin County Civil Grand Jury issued a scathing report about SMART. The report followed extensive diligence. Jurors interviewed SMART board members, staff, consultants, and contractors. They interviewed regional and local elected officials and individuals representing opinions or organizations that supported and opposed SMART. They attended SMART board meetings, reviewed print and online information including budgets, business plans, environmental impact reports, and internal SMART documentation. And they studied other San Francisco Bay Area transit systems and their related communities for comparative purposes.

That extraordinary diligence produced eleven findings and eight recommendations on a wide range of subjects: legislative, administrative, financial, operational, and public accountability. The grand jury concluded that SMART faced "overwhelming obstacles" and urged its "Board to provide the leadership required to surmount these significant challenges."[47]

"Since passage of Measure Q, there has been an economic downturn and a subsequent reduction in anticipated sales tax revenues. In addition, there are increased construction cost estimates and other contingencies, which have raised the projected costs of the project by approximately 9%. The original funding plan projected sales tax revenues of $890.7 million over the 20-year period. SMART is now looking at a shortfall of approximately $155 million. It has yet to identify, or even discuss, an alternative to the original plan."[48]

The grand jury also pointed out that SMART relied on outdated ridership estimates that, even if correct, failed to provide "significant inter-county traffic congestion relief," that "the projected ridership numbers simply do not support the popular image of a significant shift from using Highway 101 for travel between Sonoma and Marin. The bulk of the current ridership estimate will utilize SMART to travel between a handful of stations between Petaluma and Windsor, a distance of 26 miles."[49] That observation, which we'll explore in more depth later, addressed SMART's failure to understand the relevant demographics, who would be its riders, and where jobs were located in the two counties, which undermined its assumptions about traffic congestion reduction, a flaw that would become its Achilles' heel.

Mike Arnold, cochairman of Marin Citizens for Effective Transportation, distilled this weakness to a failure to ask the right question. He explained that rather than asking, "How do we pass a tax measure," proponents of the rail line should ask, "How can we solve the worsening congestion on Highway 101?"[50] The former speaks to how to play the political game, the latter to how to devise sound and thoughtful solutions to pressing local transportation problems.

The grand jury report expanded on this perspective, noting a systemic flaw in the SMART system, which would become its Achilles' heel:

> The SMART line is projected to run 70 miles through relatively lightly populated regions with a lower concentration of commerce than in the East and South Bay areas. Considering the foregoing regional scenario and comparing it with SMART's projected territory, it is not clear how SMART will be viable.
>
> Most successful rail projects today enjoy robust and dense population and employment demographics, e.g. BART and Caltrain. Targeting and serving major employers,

> airports, sports and entertainment complexes, and promoting transit-oriented development, are examples of key strategies in attracting ridership. As of today, the SMART train ridership projections account for less than one percent of the trips between Sonoma and Marin.[51]

The grand jury made another related finding, that "it was not clear that SMART will be able to be competitive with other transit options in the SMART corridor."[52] In other words, in addition to SMART's questionable ability to draw any cars off Highway 101, it faced the problem of not filling seats because public transportation commuters preferred well-established local transit options. That, the grand jury concluded, raised serious challenges to SMART's long-term sustainability.

Would SMART heed the call?

For the most part, SMART gave the grand jury the back of its hand.

In their formal response, SMART embraced the no-brainers, e.g., regurgitating the words the legislature used to establish the special district or acknowledging the skill levels and experiences of their staff.[53] Their tune changed, however, when it came to substantive matters.

For example, SMART became defensive in areas where they had not performed adequately. One finding stated that SMART had failed to identify or publicly discuss phasing or limiting the scope should adequate funding *not* be obtained. SMART did not quarrel with the omission, but rather than agree and promise change, they "partially disagreed," offering excuses for their inaction. Similarly, recall that the grand jury concluded SMART was using outdated ridership numbers. SMART admitted the data obsolescence, but, again, rather than "agree" with the finding, "partially disagreed," saying something vague about "reworking" the numbers.

SMART also outright rejected the recommendation that they undergo an *independent* audit, taking haven in the regular oversight they receive from agencies that help fund its operations. SMART also refused to delay construction of the bike and pedestrian path, which the grand jury thought ill-advised because of SMART's perilous finances. They also declined to expand the scope and membership of the citizen committee set up to oversee and keep SMART accountable.[54]

In fairness, civil grand jury recommendations are just that: recommendations. Their recipients are free, technically, to ignore them. But that in one way makes them more meaningful. The freedom to choose—in contrast to required implementation of top-down directives—tests the willingness to be self-critical, admit mistakes, be accountable, and improve performance. After all, as any fair reading of the 2010 Marin Civil Grand Jury Report would conclude, the findings and recommendations sprang from an impressive display of diligence and thoughtfulness of citizens with no axe to grind other than to serve the public interest. Indeed, it is conceivable, if not likely, that the grand jury's groundwork eclipsed what any individual or group had done previously to address and understand the issues SMART faced. The grand jury mined the depths of the local landscape, looking at all angles and sides, exhaustively drilling down to understand and deliver invaluable input, arguably rendering them better informed than any SMART proponent.

The grand jury gifted SMART a unique opportunity to up their game. Again, that doesn't mean that SMART leadership was duty-bound to implement grand jury recommendations. But it does mean that the 2010 Marin Grand Jury Report (and the many grand jury reports that would follow in later years) were litmus tests of SMART accountability.

The refusal to bend might have a structural foundation. In creating the SMART special district, the legislature adopted the preferences of local political leaders to structure SMART as a Joint Powers Authority (JPA), which allows two or more public agencies to jointly exercise common powers. In this case, the legislature directed that SMART board members be appointed from various *existing* elected positions in Sonoma and Marin counties and the Golden Gate Bridge Highway and Transportation District (GGHTD). Therein may lie the rub. How many politicians, especially in the prevailing polarized political climate, are open to a critique from nameless citizens, regardless of their "grand jury" imprimatur, that scrutinizes their performance and tells them how to get their act together?

No wonder then that the SMART board did not respond with palpable enthusiasm to what the 2010 Marin Civil Grand Jury report had to say, a line-in-the-sand mentality heralding a contentious relationship between SMART and several later civil grand juries sitting in Marin and Sonoma counties. While as will be seen, agreement sometimes will occur around the edges, by and large the SMART board made it clear they did not want any grand jury, no matter how well intentioned and exhaustively informed, telling them what to do, an entrenched arrogance that stonewalled meaningful criticism, feedback, and attempts to hold SMART accountable. That would change, as later discussed, when SMART found themselves in deep trouble as a going concern.

So for SMART, riding the wave of their Measure Q ballot victory, despite the 2010 Marin County Grand Jury Report, it was business as usual, a stance that would prove costly in the public arena. As detailed in the prologue, not only did voters reject Measure I in 2020, which sought to extend the existing quarter-cent sales tax approved in 2008 via Measure Q for an additional period of thirty years, they did so resoundingly (thirteen percentage points under the required threshold). By that time, in addition to the quality of the competing campaigns, one based in fact, the other drenched in ad hominem zeal, voters had access to a more informative history, the chance to observe consistently empty train cars and witness in the light of day an agency that defied fiscal accountability.

Credibility would soon become a major public issue for SMART. How much of what SMART advertised was fake news? How much hyperbole? What relevant data, if any, did SMART and their advocates hide from the public eye?

The emerging picture was not pretty.

3

The SMART (Mis)information Campaign

Cynics and purveyors of fake news aside, most people presumably believe voters are entitled to complete and accurate information whenever asked to cast a ballot, especially when the ask is for their money. Perhaps in today's polarized world, that expectation betrays a Pollyannaish preoccupation. But it is difficult to make the case that it isn't the right thing to do. In basic commercial terms, if the public is buying something, it ought to know what it's buying.

But SMART's public statements have often differed significantly from documented performance. It is unclear whether this comes from unchecked enthusiasm, market puffery, ineptness, or something worse. Nor is it excusable to dismiss factual inaccuracy as politics as usual or the rabid workings of the spin factory, no matter how pervasive those behaviors have become.

It many ways, it is as if SMART perceives itself a zealous advocate, dealing with the public like trial attorneys deal with judges and juries, their sole purpose to persuade and in the process ignore or downplay whatever harms the cause. "Just win, baby," to borrow the legendary rally cry of the late Al Davis, then-owner of the Oakland Raiders. SMART seems to have forgotten, however, or never understood, that they are a public servant, a privileged calling that exalts transparency, accountability, and candor above all.

Here is but one example of how SMART approached its role more as an advocate seeking to win than a public agency seeking to serve.

In April 2021, a *Press Democrat* reporter wrote that SMART "steadfastly refused to disclose more detailed daily ridership numbers. When it finally did so under mounting public pressure in late 2019, the figures obtained by *The Press Democrat* showed a 30 percent drop in weekend ridership from the first full year of service to the second, resulting in an overall drop of 2.2 percent during that period. "Until then, SMART had not provided data to the public or its governing board showing any declines in ridership."[55]

SMART has offered inaccurate or incomplete information to win over voters, who depend heavily on how proponents of ballot measures like SMART present their message. For example, apart from what economists call "rational ignorance," where voter frustration about the utility of their vote overcomes their desire to become informed, most participating voters do not peruse ballot measures like they might materials for a licensing exam or a test required for a job. Campaign literature can overwhelm and confuse, especially if you assume voters have limited attention spans. Doing the right thing by voters means prioritizing quality campaign literature presented effectively.

Consider what SMART said and did not say and what they should have said to the voting public regarding the 2006 and 2008 ballot measures (R and Q) and subsequent activities, in four areas of the rail project: (1) ridership and traffic congestion relief, (2) project costs, (3) train operations, and (4) environmental benefits.

1. **Ridership and Traffic Congestion Relief**

The foundation on which the entire SMART project rests, and the sine qua non of its sales tax measure campaigns, is that the rail line will make a substantial dent in Highway 101 traffic congestion during peak hours. Anyone driving north on Highway 101 during the morning on weekdays in Marin and Sonoma counties gets a frontal look at other drivers suffering mind-numbing gridlock in the opposite direction, a logjam that replicates for drivers who grind their way north at end of the day.

An unqualified promise to solve that problem with a cutting-edge solution can be inebriating. Time and again, SMART has boasted supreme confidence to achieve that lofty goal, often resorting to far-reaching hyperbole.

For example, in one of their eighteen 2008 White Papers, it categorically stated:

> SMART *will* provide an alternative to 101 for *commuters who now have no choice*. Whether they are travelling from Windsor to Santa Rosa or Novato to San Rafael or the length of the line from Cloverdale to Larkspur, the train will give them a *faster*, *less polluting*, more relaxing and should they choose to use their commute time for work—more productive commute than they could have in a car.[56] (Emphasis added)

That same year, in a July White Paper, SMART stepped it up a notch, touting the "*transformative* ability of SMART to become the *backbone* of a *complete* alternative transportation system that links thousands of residents to a network of buses, shuttles and ferries."[57] (Emphasis added.)

Trains Magazine attributed similar grandiose statements, first to the general manager of SMART (Lillian Hames), "In five years, we're delivering a *major railroad to 750,000 people* who have no option other than 'parking lot,'" and next to a SMART director, "SMART train service will be transformative for the North Bay . . . *a game changer*—a smart transportation option that will *enhance our quality of life period*."[58] (Emphasis added.)

The facts, however, told (and continue to tell) a different story.

For example, the SMART EIR (completed in 2006), after stating that "2010 rail ridership would be approximately 5,300 per average weekday,"—a number SMART later reduced—went on to say: "Although the proposed project provides reduction in 2010 volumes in certain areas, the oversaturation of demand in the corridor often causes freeway volume to fill back up to the original level. *Much of the traffic congestion relief would be found on surface streets paralleling Highway 101, rather than on the freeway itself*."[59] (Emphasis added.)

That conclusion has a sound basis. Taking the projections SMART declared at face value, the numbers are entirely unremarkable when broken down.

The reference to 5,300 is *round* trips, thus encompassing the same drivers and cars twice. Half of 5,300 trips leaves 2,650 riders, two-thirds of which were expected to be Sonoma County residents en route to Marin County, one-third going in the opposite direction. Two-thirds of 2,650 leaves 1,775. Further, not all of those commuters are coming out of cars. In absolute numbers, the impact on traffic congestion is negligible. But there is more—or more aptly, less.

Consider that in 2017, according to Caltrans Ramp Volume reports, Highway 101 experienced at least 1.5 million vehicle trips each day between Airport Blvd (near SMART's northern terminus) and Sir Francis Drake Blvd (SMART's southern terminus after completing the Larkspur extension). The SMART Annual Report in December 2017 stated: "In 2017, SMART carried a total of 252,295 passengers with a daily average of 2,191 on weekdays and 1,393 on weekends."[60]

Even rounding up to three thousand riders per weekday *and* assuming that each of them came out of cars driving on Highway 101 for the same purpose as riding the train, SMART train ridership would constitute only **0.002 percent** of the total Highway 101 vehicle trips. For purposes of quantifying potential reduction of traffic congestion, the impact is zero (in exchange for over $1 billion). You'll never see that breakdown in any SMART literature.

Indeed, the Marin Conservation League pointed this out to SMART in September 2006, to no avail:

> SMART will only reduce vehicular miles traveled in Sonoma-Marin by 3/100 of 1%. . . . Less than 1% of the residents of Sonoma and Marin would be the daily users of this $1.4 billion SMART project. We note that 2.5 million trips are made in Sonoma and Marin every weekday, yet SMART's EIR projects it will carry only 5,050 passenger trips. Marin County Transit District bus services carry nearly 10 times more Marin riders than will SMART.[61]

Further, the SMART EIR projected that in 2025—at which point SMART was supposed to have been up and running for about fifteen years—over 25,000 Sonoma County residents would work in Marin County and, of them, only 230 would take the morning trains during peak hours to Marin. The EIR also projected that only 500 Marin residents would take the train each day.

There was another problem with the SMART numbers. In all of their public documents, including what they put into the public domain to support ballot measures, SMART projected total ridership usage, *not merely peak hours* of home-to-work and work-to-home riders. By doing so, it implied to the public that the number it used—5,300 daily (and later 5,046) and 1.5 million annually—were peak riders its train would eliminate to reduce traffic congestion. By including projected non-peak ridership, SMART skewed what they told the public.

SMART did not pay heed to anything bearing on the traffic and ridership numbers that undermined their coveted representations. On the contrary. They buried all of it. Nowhere is there, for example, any SMART public statement placing projected ridership within a frame of comparative reference like total Highway 101 riders during peak hours. Rather, SMART took refuge consistently in terms like "5,300 cars a day" and "1.5 million cars annually" to whet the appetite of the taxpayer, key words calculated to become a refrain that could help them *win*. Bragging that it would pull 1.5 million riders in future years off Highway 101 is facially tantalizing for sure. But it is a gross distortion of the facts and the traffic impact, and injurious to the public.

None of this should come as a surprise to anyone who understands the utter pointlessness of rail service within suburbia. It is a pipe dream for a simple reason: intra-suburban passenger rail does not serve major employment centers. This has to do with what is called the triple substitution effect, a fancy scientific way for describing basic human driving choices: time, route, and mode.

SMART has from the start ignored the inherent limitations of their ambitious project, which their consistently misleading statements reflect, fooling taxpayers into thinking local passenger rail is the panacea for traffic reduction and associated environmental problems.

Further, the representation that the SMART train is a "faster" alternative is also not accurate and deserves comment. By calling *the train* "faster," SMART is comparing apples—the time spent in the car when using Highway 101 to get from home to work—with oranges—the time sitting in the train. It ignores the first- and last-mile segments of train usage. The actual SMART trip begins at home, not at a SMART station, typically in a car that takes the commuter *to* the station and ends at a destination that commonly requires the rider to take a shuttle, a bus, or to walk to the final destination (e.g., the workplace). By ignoring that not so insignificant part of travel, SMART misleads when it labels the train a "faster" alternative. In the real world, not the imagined world SMART wants taxpayers to inhabit, trip duration means "total trip length." The SMART train, as a result, is not only not faster but more cumbersome since the train commute gets parsed into segments of "on and off." That is why a within-suburban rail system takes so few passengers.

When it comes to ridership and Highway 101 cars, SMART has glorified low meaningless numbers. To put it colloquially, there ain't no there, there.

2. Project Costs

The constantly escalating cost of the SMART project is staggering, albeit not unusual for public transit investments. While that cost is now out in the open, it has not always been. The representations SMART made about the cost of the rail project to persuade taxpayers to provide what SMART categorized as the bulk of project funding were both a moving target and misleading.

In its 2006 Measure R household mailer, SMART boasted that: "SMART is at least four times **less expensive to build**, operate and maintain than building and maintaining highways."[62] (Bold in original.)

First, that statement is a silly and woefully unhelpful and incomplete hypothetical. Is SMART comparing itself with massive projects like the Big Dig in Boston, the San Francisco-Oakland Bay Bridge East Span Replacement, or the Alaskan Way Viaduct Replacement Tunnel in Seattle? And if so, why do we care how well SMART compares to projects that are entirely or mostly dissimilar?

Second, the comparison is a red herring. The issue SMART faced from the start and continues to labor under is not whether it will cost more or less than building a highway including operating costs, but whether their claimed benefits justify the massive costs. What does it matter if the train project costs less than building a highway if it does not deliver on its promises?

But taking SMART up on cost comparison, consider the comments of the Marin Conservation League, which said that same year: "SMART's average Operating Cost per passenger for the [twenty-year period of the sales tax] will be over three times the average of all other transit systems in the Bay Area."[63] And, in a more realistic apples-to-apples comparison than rail to highway construction, and contrary to its boast as a visionary "transformative" transportation system, data in 2006 projected SMART as the *most expensive* transportation system out of a total of eleven Bay Area systems, including Muni-Bus, Muni-Light Rail, ACT Transit, BART, Muni-Cable Car, SamTrans, Caltrain, GGT-Bus, GGT-Ferry, and ACE. SMART registered in at an annual cost of $20.35

per passenger. The others ranged from $2 to $15 with an average of $6.26.

It also helps to understand how SMART likes to *present* financial information whenever they want to curry favor with taxpayers.

In its 2006 Expenditure Plan for Measure R, SMART forecast project costs for the rail line and proposed bike and pedestrian pathway at $433 million, with annual operating costs at $16.25 million.[64] They also estimated annual revenues of $33 million and said the public should assume it would be burdened with—via a combination of the sales tax and commuter fares—75 percent of total costs, 66 percent from the tax and 9 percent from fares. SMART also told the public that revenue from fares would constitute *30 percent of annual operating costs* ("farebox recovery"). These numbers assumed commencement of train operations in 2009–2010.[65]

The $433 million number was grossly misleading and cleverly so.

SMART included a table (Table 1) in the 2006 Expenditure Plan titled, "SMART Project Costs." It had two sections: "Project Capital Costs" and "*Annual* Operating Costs" (emphasis added). The first included the $433 million number (a combination of Project Rail of $337 million and Bicycle Pedestrian Pathway of $46 million) and the second, a total $16.25 million, was comprised of three items: "Rail Project, Bicycle Pedestrian Pathway, and Shuttle Services." SMART did not, however, provide the aggregate number for operating expenses—i.e., twenty years times $16.25 million = $325 million—which would bring total "SMART Project Costs" to at least $764,300,000.[66] Why not? In contrast, they saw fit to proudly tell the public, first at the top of the Expenditure Plan, and twice more later, how much *revenue* they would collect from taxpayers over the twenty-year period ($668 million).[67]

But they did not want to highlight for voters the other side of the ledger, the total costs of the project.

Further, titling the table "SMART Project Costs" implies *total* costs. But making that assumption, it turned out, would lead voters astray. That is because buried further in the Expenditure Plan, on page 7, the penultimate page, is yet another table (Table 2). It is titled "Anticipated Costs and Revenues Over 20 Years (Millions $)." It *differs* from the prior table. Table 2 includes line items for the "rail project, pathway, district operations, and program contingency" with these costs: "$387, $46, $874, and $93," respectively, for total of $1,400. At the top of the table, as noted, it states the numbers are in "Millions $."[68] Nowhere does SMART mention the literal number of **$1.4 billion** or explain the differences between the two tables.

SMART knew it is the rare voter, if any, who will wade through the morass of the voting pamphlet to land at the Expenditure Plan. SMART also knew that if any voter even made it to Table 1, they wouldn't perform calculations to arrive at $764.3 million. SMART decision-makers were wise enough to know only the rarely would voters survive that process to land at Table 2 and even if they did, would only eyeball the line item with the total of "$1,400," potentially missing that the true forecasted cost of the project over the twenty-year tax collection period was $1.4 billion.

SMART easily could have inserted into the narrative content, had they wanted, a single sentence that informed voters of the true total project cost over the twenty-year tax period, e.g., "The total project costs, including capital costs, operating expenses, district operations, and contingencies, over the twenty-year taxation period, is projected to be $1.4 billion." They chose not to, while three times doing the opposite to exalt the gross amount of projected revenues over the same period.

The Expenditure Plan financial data presentation was the antithesis of voter-friendly.

Further, in July 2008, in one of their eighteen "White Papers," SMART stated: "Passenger fares will cover *more than a third* of the train's operating costs—a 'farebox recovery' rate that compares well with other transit systems throughout the United States." (emphasis added).[69] Farebox recovery is the percentage of operating expense that collected rider fares offsets.

First, SMART had no reasonable basis for this projection. The National Transit Data base, which the Federal Transit Administration maintains, shows that in 2007 the average farebox recovery for the smaller and more comparable national commuter rail systems that reported was 25 percent.[70] SMART chose 36 percent, significantly higher.

Second, those projections turned out to be wildly off the mark.

For example, SMART's farebox recoveries in 2019, 2020, 2021, and 2022 were 15 percent, 11 percent, 3 percent, and 5 percent, respectively.

By way of comparison, as of January 1, 2020, farebox recovery percentage rates for the local transit systems serving Sonoma and Marin counties ran from a high of 56.9 to a low of 6.5, with SMART coming in near the bottom at 10.8:

(56.9, 53.1, 37.1, 11.1, **10.8 (SMART)**, 10.4, 8.8, 8.7, 8.3, 7.5, and 6.5).

Similarly, on January 2021, the percentages ran from a high of 57.3 to a low of 1.3, with SMART coming in, again, hugging the bottom, at 2.8:

(57.3, 8.1, 7.3, 6.3, 3.8, 3.3, **2.8 (SMART)**, 2.4, 2.2, 1.7. and 1.3).

SMART's farebox revenue rates are mediocre at best and meagre at worst.

In its 2008 Expenditure Plan for Measure Q, SMART repeated its inflated projection of farebox recovery, this time at 36 percent.[71] It also increased total project costs to $541 million (including the proposed bike and pedestrian path), a **25 percent increase.**[72] SMART further represented that the combination of sales tax revenues and commuter fares would account for 78percent of revenues, 66 percent of the former and 12 percent of the latter (up from 9 percent).[73] It estimated annual operating costs at $19.3 million, an **increase of 19 percent.**[74] In a separate 2008 document titled "Funding Plan," SMART stated that project costs would be $589.2 million.[75]

Again, both numbers, $541 and $589 million, were grossly misleading in the same way as the 2006 Expenditure Plan. SMART included the identical table that focused only on "Annual Operating Costs." Based on that table, the *total* project costs, capital costs, and operating expenses over a twenty-year period amounted to $927 million ($541 million in capital costs and $386,000,000 in twenty-year operating expenses (if you do the math). And, like the 2006 Expenditure Plan, SMART mentioned the twenty-year number for *revenues* three times ($890 million) but omitted mention of the comparable number for total costs. And arguably worse than what they did in their 2006 Expenditure Plan, they *excluded* Table 2 and mentioned the billion dollar number one time in passing: "an estimated 20-year investment of nearly $1.4 billion" with no breakdown or explanation.

SMART also changed the launch date in the two years between Measures R and Q to 2014, a four-year delay. Full service did not commence until August 2017.

***

The economy nosedived in 2008 following the collapse of Lehman Brothers, adversely impacting SMART's anticipated sales tax revenues from Measure Q. It also revealed how poorly SMART had prepared financially for building out the project.

The sales tax reduction denied SMART sufficient revenues to finance the construction bond needed to build a 70-mile rail line, leaving them with one option: *phase* the project. SMART described the dilemma in its 2010 Annual Report:

> Due to the severe economic downturn that began in the Fall of 2008 and continued into 2009, revenue projections were significantly lower for the Strategic Plan than previously forecast in the SMART Funding Plan and Expenditure Plan, which had been developed a year earlier. Total sales tax revenues from the Measure Q Program were estimated in the Strategic Plan to be approximately $845 million over 20 years, a reduction of 5.2% from the estimate in 2008. Most significantly, SMART's bonding capacity was reduced by $100 million due to lower sales tax revenue projections and changed conditions in the bond market. Meanwhile, cost projections were adjusted upward by about 11 percent to reflect increased contingencies, higher vehicle costs and added project scope.
>
> These changes resulted in a Strategic Plan that identified a funding gap in the project. To preserve the plan to build a complete 70-mile train and pathway project with passenger train service operating by Fall 2014, the Plan acknowledged a shortfall of $155 million (in 2008$), or $175 million in inflated dollars.[76]

SMART quantified the funding gap at $109 million for the phase one segment from Santa Rosa to San Rafael, then eliminated $88 million of that shortfall by deferring and eliminating certain costs, reducing the funding gap to $21 million. SMART or someone on their behalf devised a plan to target three local agencies for bailout funding: the Transportation Authority of Marin (TAM) ($8 million), the Metropolitan Transportation Commission (MTC) ($10 million), and the Sonoma County Transportation Authority (SCTA) ($3 million). Each had to approve the gap funding for SMART to receive any. The SCTA, with no fanfare, approved the funding in early June.

TAM put the funding item on its agenda at its June 23 commission meeting.[77] Prior to June 23, 2011, information circulated that the financials SMART was using to entice agency contributions had omitted $35 million in costs, about 10 percent of phase one of the project. For some reason, that did not become an issue at the June 23 meeting. After its normal process, including public comment, the TAM Board of Commissions voted 7–7 on the motion to provide SMART the $8 million. As a result, the motion failed.[78]

The commission recessed before taking up other agenda items. During the recess, a TAM board commissioner who voted in favor of the motion apparently had a sidebar with a board commissioner who voted against the measure. After the recess, the nay voting commissioner requested that the board entertain a motion for reconsideration. After conferring with counsel about the legalities of taking such action, the commission said it would entertain a seconded motion for reconsideration. The motion passed 8–6, the pivotal vote coming from the commissioner who had a change of heart during the short recess.[79]

On June 30, with two of the three agency approvals in hand, SMART disclosed to MTC that they had worked up three interim progress reports (IPRs), financial documents designed to show a balanced budget with full funding of phase one of construction: two were for internal use and one was for "public hearing" consumption. The internal IPRs included the infamous $35 million cost item (and thus a balanced budget), while the "public hearing" version excluded the $35 million (showing an unbalanced budget).[80]

The TAM board met again on July 7. For reasons that are unclear, the meeting agenda included whether the commission should entertain a motion to "rescind" the 8–6 vote cast on June 23.[81] During the discussion that followed, and after public comment, a commissioner confronted the SMART GM about the $35 million missing item. The GM, astonishingly, first disclaimed any knowledge. When pressed, he delivered a rambling response, talking about "turning wheels" in the construction business, but not a responsive answer, which prompted a follow-up question from the curious commissioner. When asked a third time, the SMART GM denied any omission of the $35 million, even though SMART was on record with MTC about the missing cost item, which, according to the inquiring commissioner, had gone "viral."[82] It was as if everyone knew about the missing item except the SMART GM. Yet, despite troubling questions about whether SMART had cooked their books, the TAM Commission voted 8–4–1 against the motion to rescind, keeping in place the "reconsidered" decision of June 23.[83]

SMART gamesmanship continued before MTC.

As part of their effort to procure an MTC contribution, SMART claimed substantial savings based on an agreement with the Northwest Pacific Railroad (NWP), which handles freight operations on the same rail line SMART uses. According to SMART, their agreement with NWP eliminated freight use of the rail line during the SMART construction period, bringing a savings of $10 million and helping to balance the phase one budget. Apparently, however, NWP had not entered into such an agreement with SMART and the $10 million purported savings were questionable.

SMART also claimed to have "found revenue" of $11 million from an arbitrary increase in projected sales tax growth rate. The issue was that the growth rate SMART used conflicted with what MTC had determined was reasonable. In other words, SMART arbitrarily increased the projected revenues, burying the number in their financials, trying to slip it by MTC, again to appear fully funded and thus using a balanced budget.

SMART also identified a $12 million savings from lower operations and maintenance costs over the course of a substantial period of time. But upon inspection, it became clear that SMART had not adjusted the number for present value, misstating their financials and proposed budget by $6.1 million.

SMART nonetheless won MTC over and got the bailout funds. Politicians will do what politicians do. But SMART had again showed that their financial numbers could not be taken at face value and that the public would be well-served to cast a consistently skeptical eye on whatever data SMART put out.

3. Train Operations

One of the most formidable obstacles SMART has faced is not only the lack of a major employment center to serve, but low population density, which limits the effectiveness of the rail line. SMART never talks about that. Others have, however.

The Marin Conservation League noted in 2006:

> The proposed SMART project only connects relatively low population density suburban cities of Sonoma and Marin, unlike other Metropolitan rail systems. Direct service to and from Central City areas of greater population density and concentrated employment centers is essential to

> generate ridership; over 80% of BART riders, for example, are to or from downtown San Francisco or Oakland. In addition, the proposed Larkspur station site for SMART is a 10-minute walk to the Larkspur Ferry Terminal. This gap in connectivity for travel to and from San Francisco is inconvenient, subjects riders to travel delays, and is unattractive for commuters.
>
> Residents of Central, South, and West Marin have little reason to use SMART for their travel needs within and between the two counties, or to go to San Francisco. Likewise the residents of the Western and Eastern areas of Sonoma County are also located too far from SMART to make it a useful transportation choice.[84]

An even greater operational problem is the first and last mile. Again, the first and last mile signifies the distance commuters must cover getting to their transit departure station and from the transit destination station before making their way to their final destination. The SMART infrastructure does not connect people to destinations in either direction. Unlike most round-trips in a car, SMART commuters need a car or a bus to get to a station to commence their commute and some transit help at the other end to get to their destinations. It has plagued and continues to plague the rail system.

As the Marin County Grand Jury noted in its June 2023 report:

> SMART is a system that, in contrast to other Bay Area transit agencies, has fewer potential riders, operates on a route with stops that are not close to many residences or large employment centers, and its route is such that it does not serve as many commuters as do other public transit agencies.[85]

Larkspur is a case in point. Here is how SMART has whitewashed the problem.

"The Larkspur Ferry Terminal is just a few minutes' walk from the SMART rail station, making this station a good destination for those headed to San Francisco. For those who are unable or would prefer not to walk to the ferry, SMART will offer a free shuttle connecting the rail station to the ferry terminal."[86]

Tell that to riders who have to walk from the terminal on one side of Highway 101 and navigate their way to the other side before getting to the ferry. The train leaves commuters across the way from the Country Mart *on the other side of Sir Francis Drake Blvd.* It is a trek, hardly "a few minute" stroll or pleasant walk. To make matters worse, the ferry and SMART schedules are not synced, adding a wait time for anyone traveling to San Francisco. SMART buried these inefficiencies. SMART has added some shuttles, but the omission there is that SMART did not price them as part of their financial calculations.

The Marin Civil Grand Jury in April 2019 made this finding:

> The distance between the SMART Larkspur terminal and the ferry terminal may act as a barrier that could adversely impact SMART ridership since currently there are no known plans for public transit between the two terminals.[87]

4. Environmental Impact

SMART's environmental claims bootstrapped from its interrelated claims of ridership and removing cars from Highway 101. For example, here is a typical SMART assertion:

> As noted in SMART's Final Environmental Impact Report, by **replacing more than 5,000 vehicle trips per day with rides**

> **on rail cars powered by modern clean-diesel fuels,** SMART will prevent more than 30 million pounds of greenhouse gases from entering our air each year. That's equivalent to removing 50,000 cars *completely off our roads* in the first 20 years of the train's operation, according to the U.S. Environmental Protection Agency.[88] (Emphasis in original; bold added.)

Thus, the claimed environmental impact turns exclusively on, and is in direct proportion to, SMART's ability to reduce traffic congestion. If the latter does not pan out, if there is de minimis or no reduction in traffic congestion, the environmental benefits are questionable. Worse, and ironically, if SMART has not pulled an appreciable number of drivers off the road—and so far in that regard, it has been a dismal failure—the diesel-powered trains will have *added* to greenhouse gases, thus worsening air quality in Marin and Sonoma counties.

Putting aside the entwined relationship between riders and traffic reduction and environmental impact, the evidence suggests that the environmental claims SMART makes have been misleading. SMART likely knows that environmental sensitivity in the Bay Area is probably as acute as any other place in the country. Teasing the local voting constituency with provocative claims about climate change and greenhouse gases and a better life for all is preaching to the choir. Hence, SMART has been prone to make seemingly unqualified and sweeping statements.

For example, in a letter dated May 30, 2008, in an effort to raise campaign funds, the chair of the SMART board of directors claimed that approval of Measure Q was an "opportunity" to "*save our planet.*" (Emphasis added.)

In a February 2008 White Paper, SMART claimed that their "clean, fast trains will reduce greenhouse gas emissions by about 31 million pounds a year, according to the project's Environmental Impact Report."[89] But a mere three months later, in May, in their project description, SMART substantially altered the data: "The rail project will . . . reduce greenhouse gases, which contribute to global warming, by at least 124,000 pounds per day." That translates to *45 million pounds a year*, 14 million more than previously claimed earlier that year, almost 50 percent greater.[90]

Also that year, in a February 2008 White Paper, SMART made this claim:

> Sonoma-Marin Area Rail Transit will provide the cleanest, most up-to-date and most practical rail technology available to the North Bay. . . .With these new technologies, diesel doesn't have to be a dirty word. The combination of 21st Century fuels, catalytic systems and particulate traps will make the SMART train one of the cleanest ways to travel in Sonoma and Marin counties.[91]

But if transparent and frank, SMART would not, nor could they, deny that diesel engines emit greenhouse gases. Here is how the Marin Conservation League (MCL) described them:

> Pollutants and greenhouse gas emissions from the operations of SMART would be less than that of auto use by the projected train riders. However, it would not be any better than other transportation alternatives such as express buses, car and van pooling on HOV lanes, and hybrid local buses. Alternative transit options can achieve the same pollution reduction and emission results at far less cost per passenger. The planned widening of Highway 101 in the Narrows between Novato and Petaluma with HOV lanes will provide an alternative express bus route to SMART.[92]

And, on September 28, 2006, the *San Francisco Chronicle*, under the banner of "PROPOSITION 65 WARNING," in discussing diesel exhaust from rail operations, wrote: "Diesel exhaust is a chemical known to the state of California to cause cancer, and contains chemicals known to the state to cause birth defects or other reproductive harm."

SMART also failed to highlight for the public how the rail line would impact wetland wildlife habitats. As the Marin Conservation League stated: "Inclusion of the Bike and Pedestrian Path alongside SMART will require increasing the footprint of the right-of-way and encroach upon sensitive wetlands. In addition, the construction and operation of SMART along the right-of-way will degrade wetland habitats along its route and impair the ability of wildlife to travel between the wetlands and needed neighboring upland habitats."[93]

One glaring omission in all the SMART environmental statements is the failure to account for how current and anticipated technological advances in the automobile engine will shape the future of transportation, locally and elsewhere. Demand for electric cars is robust. Goldman Sachs research recently commented: "We expect the automobile industry to undergo a major transformation between 2020 and 2030, driven by the increasing adoption of vehicle electrification and autonomous driving." It added that by 2040, the share of electric car sales would be "well over 80% in many developed countries."[94]

In terms of environmental impact, the electrical car is a mode of transportation vastly superior to the SMART train: a virtually net-zero carbon emitter vs. a carbon emitter. SMART has utterly ignored this.

SMART also swept under the rug the increase of gas emissions from those cars and buses that take its riders to and from SMART stations, part of the first- and last-mile segments.

Consider too the intra-county congestion the SMART train causes, introducing idling engines into the mix whenever stopping to allow passage of the trains. SMART chose not to account for this in its environmental calculations in the rush to bathe the public with favorable data.

SMART's environmental case is unconvincing and incomplete. SMART has never accounted for improvements in the auto engine. It has never accounted for the drive to the parking lot. It has never accounted for the congestion and idle engines it causes in San Rafael. It has never accounted for the percentage of riders who have and who will switch from bus transit. And it has never accounted for the true emissions of the diesel engines.

The greenhouse gas emission issue is a political carrot SMART has used to lure voters into a false sense of environmental progress. Even if SMART were able to fulfill its promise of moving sufficient numbers of cars off the road, the net benefit to the environment is negligible. Touting environmental change is a ruse to make voters believe that the rail line will meaningfully improve the air they breathe. At most, the impact is, as the cliché goes, a mere drop in the ocean that does not justify any appreciable portion of SMART's staggering cost.

***

SMART's win-win advocacy approach in lieu of a public servant mentality of completeness and accuracy has done a disturbing disservice to local communities. If SMART does anything else down the road, assuming it has a road available, it would be well advised to embrace and regularly showcase an unwavering accountability, uncompromising accuracy, and unflinching transparency, and be bold and honest enough to let the chips fall where they may.

4

An Ethical Conundrum

Can Taxpayers Trust *The Press Democrat*?

Voters can rely on various sources to guide them toward ballot decisions. For one, they can scan voting pamphlets to see who is lining up for and who is against a measure, a natural impulse to match personal values with those public positions, e.g., shared perspectives on the criminal justice system, funding of public education, and taxation.

Voters can also fixate on word choice in ballot measures. A study published in *Social Science Quarterly* in November 2021 explored whether select ballot wording shapes voting behavior, finding, for example, that voters were more disposed to support a tax increase described as an additional "two cents per dollar" than a quantified percentage increase. Similarly, use of the word "green" to describe a project, apart from whether a measure has substantive merits, can rouse environmental sensibilities and drive voters to check "yes" on the ballot sheet.[95]

Then there is the sway of local media.

One twenty-year study of ballot measures, published in the *State Politics & Policy Quarterly* in March 2018, identified a link between local newspaper endorsements of specific ballot measures and a lower percentage of voters rejecting them. That should not be surprising. Local newspapers with a circumscribed circulation can be a tie that binds a community, as they are uniquely situated to cover a wide range of subjects of local interest and give residents a sense of engagement and belonging.[96]

It follows that editorial boards are well-reminded they can wield enormous power over public thinking and that their readership is likely to trust what they have to say. That sacred trust is acute within a relatively small enclave like Sonoma County and can be implicated when newspaper ownership has a financial interest in a subject matter the paper covers, an ethical dilemma that came home to roost not long ago for Santa Rosa's *Press Democrat* regarding its editorial coverage of SMART. The paper found itself embroiled in a tangle of behind-the-scenes maneuvers and relationships infected with conflicts of interest where the players were scratching each other's back for financial gain.

The facts are complex. Here is a simplified version.

In 2006, a business group, including Doug Bosco, a former California state politician turned businessman with experience in transportation, formed a private enterprise named the Northwestern Pacific Railroad Company (NWP). About fifteen years earlier, California created the North Coast Railroad Authority (NCRA) to refurbish three hundred miles of Northern California rail line that had fallen into dysfunctional disarray. The Federal Railroad Administration had shut down NCRA's rail operations until the completion of requisite repairs.

The game plan positioned NWP—the for-profit private entity—to enter into a lease with NCRA—the public agency—to run a freight line operation along the refurbished line, moving lumber and agricultural products on the southern portion of the line and gravel on the northern portion. The ninety-five-year lease between NWP and NCRA featured a bizarre provision. NWP only had to pay rent to NCRA if its freight operations generated annual net revenue of $5 million (which never happened). For its part, NCRA bore full responsibility to transform the rail line from ruin into an operational infrastructure, spending hundreds of millions of public dollars in the process.

Then the plot thickened.

In 2011, Darius Anderson, a real estate developer and political lobbyist, along with Doug Bosco of NWP and others, cofounded Sonoma Media Investments, which then acquired *The Press Democrat*, among other local media outlets. Mr. Anderson also owned and headed Platinum Advisors, a political lobbying firm.[97]

That same year, NCRA and NWP commenced running freight along restored rail lines in the southern portion. Par for the course, the financial results did not match earlier projections, which forced the landlord, NCRA, to borrow money from its tenant NWP, among others, transforming the leasing relationship into a one-sided profit-generating machine for NWP. It eventually became a financial disaster for the public and a golden goose for NWP and its owners. Indeed, the California Department of Transportation (Caltrans) and the Federal Emergency Management Agency (FEMA) called the NCRA gambit a "high risk" target of state and federal funding. And a former member of the NCRA board (Bernard Meyers) made the apt observation that NCRA existed "for the benefit of its lessee" and that the public "is not getting . . . the benefits of tens of millions of taxpayer dollars used in the line's rehabilitation." He called the NCRA-NWP arrangement a "lop-sided, sweetheart deal."[98]

In an article in the *Bohemian*, dated November 3, 2021, journalist Will Caruthers summarized the NWP-NCRA relationship this way:

> A 2020 state assessment of the NCRA—in effect, an autopsy—examines how the public rail agency's intertwined relationship with the private NWP Co came to pass. Remember, the NCRA was theoretically created for the purpose of saving the publicly owned railroad, but it became, in effect, forever indebted to Bosco's privately owned company, according to government reports and a former NCRA board member.[99]

By this time as well, NWP had agreed to share the southern portion of the refurbished line with SMART, with NWP running freight and SMART, if and when it commenced operations, running passenger service, along the shared rail line.[100]

Then, in August 2015, keeping it all in the family, SMART hired Anderson (owner of *The Press Democrat*) and Platinum Advisors as its lobbying agency to find state funding and favorable legislation from the powers that be in Sacramento. Acting for SMART, Anderson's firm lobbied for a bill that would put NWP in bed with SMART and public funds in the coffers of NWP. SMART also requested that Bosco intervene on its behalf to deploy his political pull in the Sacramento effort. After much back-and-forth, the pro-SMART forces collaborating with politicians, and Bosco helping to craft acceptable legislative language, got it done.[101]

Accordingly, in 2018, Governor Jerry Brown signed the bill, codified in California Government Code § 13978.9. The avowed purpose of the new law was "to dissolve the North Coast Railroad Authority and dispense with its assets and liabilities." It did not *direct* that SMART own the freight-related assets. Rather, it directed the California State Transportation Agency to assess, among other things, "the options for the "potential transfer of the southern portion of the rail corridor," and "specific assets and liabilities" to SMART. It also authorized funding for what appeared a fait accompli transfer of power and control that spelled the death knell of NCRA and set the stage for SMART to become a freight train operator to supplement its commuter rail operations.[102]

Subsequently, with the approval of the California State Transportation Agency, SMART and NWP entered into an agreement whereby NWP transferred its freight rights and assets to SMART in exchange for $4 million of new state funds.[103]

The state later threw another $3.7 million at NCRA to repay NWP on outstanding loans the failing freight agency had with NWP.[104]

For its part, SMART used about $600,000 of its public funds to pay Anderson's Platinum Advisors for their various lobbying efforts, including at the federal level (the latter beyond the scope of the SMART-Platinum contract).

In May 2020, the SMART board approved the acquisition of the freight right-of-way with a vote of 11–0–1, the abstaining member (San Rafael mayor Gary Phillips) lamenting that the board never received data to show the profitability of the NWP freight operation. "[Taking] on this obligation with the unknowns that are present . . . [is] quite frankly . . . quite foolish of the board." He also expressed concern that SMART was ill-equipped to run a freight business.[105]

A year *after* deciding to become a freight operator, SMART hired an agency to assess the *feasibility* of its *existing* takeover from NWP and NCRA.[106]

The after-the-fact study found that SMART would have to invest substantial public resources to potentially make the freight operation a success:

> The amount of freight revenue generated on SMART's lines will be highly dependent upon the willingness of SMART to support and promote the freight business. . . . On the other hand, with restrictive policies, minimal investment, poor promotion of services, and unwillingness to host storage cars, the freight business will likely decline, providing less revenue in the future than it does today.[107]

The situation became even more complex and conflict-ridden when Anderson on behalf of SMART and Bosco on behalf of *both* NCRA and NWP became enmeshed in negotiations with a developer (Spanos Corporation) that needed rail track rights-of-way that SMART and NCRA controlled to complete a housing project in Petaluma. The dealmaking produced an easement sale that gave SMART $1.4 million and NCRA $1 million (some of which was used to repay the debt NCRA owed Bosco's NWP).

An article in the *Bohemian* on November 10, 2021 noted:

> John Pelissero, Ph.D., a senior scholar at the Markkula Center for Applied Ethics at Santa Clara University, told the *Bohemian/Pacific Sun* that the numerous overlapping interests on display during Anderson's time working for SMART raise serious ethical questions—even if it's just an appearance of a conflict of interest. "When it comes to ethical issues, it doesn't matter whether it's an intended or a perceived conflict of interest. They both present ethical problems for those who are involved. And when you're dealing with government, when you're dealing with the

> public citizens and taxpayers, that's where one really needs to pay special attention to the perception that you're acting in your role as a government agency or somebody who works for a government agency in a way that creates a conflict of interest," Pelissero said.[108]

Conflicts aside, the participants in these transactions had become one happy family: Anderson, Bosco, Platinum Advisors, *The Press Democrat*, NWP, and SMART.

Ethics

One burning question this den of self-interest presented was how to handle the conflict between the owners of *The Press Democrat*—who were financially invested in the SMART scope of operations—and its editorial coverage of the SMART project. What were or should be the governing principles?

Codes of conduct are essential for the fair and honest administration of the work of the media and journalists, a framework no less important when it comes to newspaper editorials, where the paper delivers its pearls of wisdom from a bully pulpit to a captive audience.

A newspaper editorial, of course, is an opinion, a subjective assessment of a subject matter, commonly capturing the majority or unanimous perspective of an editorial board, without attribution to a specific board member. It is designed to influence readers, persuading them to embrace or reaffirm a viewpoint, and in the case of ballot measures, propel readers to vote a certain way.

Responsible editorials engage readers professionally based on an assessment of all relevant facts without succumbing to personalities and personal interests. Readers deserve well-reasoned editorials that are balanced and free of bias, undue influence, and conflicts of interest, and not based on cherry-picked facts to advance a hidden agenda.

A PhD in journalism is not required to appreciate how media bias can affect individual and public perception on a wide range of subjects. This is especially true in the political realm, where the media is commonly the primary source of information available to readers and, as a result, can shape collective voter behavior.

The bar is heightened when it comes to conflicts of interest. Conflicts of interest can compromise judgment and cloud thinking, knowingly or unwittingly. The existence of a conflict does not, of necessity, mean an editorial board has fallen prey to bias. It does mean, however, that a responsible editorial board, pledged to act without bias, should be up front with readers about any potential or actual conflict. Editorial boards should never lose sight of their role as agents of trust, which is why responsible newspapers have codes of ethics to guide them through the thicket of editorial bias and improper appearances.

Consider, for example, the *New York Times*.

> The goal of *The New York Times* is to cover the news as impartially as possible—"without fear or favor," in the words of Adolph Ochs, our patriarch—and to treat readers, news sources, advertisers and others fairly and openly, and *to be seen to be doing so*. The reputation of *The Times* rests upon such *perceptions*, and so do the professional reputations of its staff members.[109] (Emphasis added)

In its "Conflict of Interest Policy," the *Washington Post* states:

> This newspaper is pledged to avoid conflict of interest or the appearance of conflict of interest, wherever and

> whenever possible. We have adopted stringent policies on these issues, conscious that they may be more restrictive than is customary in the world of private business. . . . All reporters and editors, wherever they may work, are required to disclose to their department head any financial interests that might be in conflict or give the appearance of a conflict in their reporting or editing duties.[110]

The Society of Professional Journalists decrees: "The highest and primary obligation of ethical journalism is to serve the public. Journalists should: Avoid conflicts of interest, real or perceived. Disclose unavoidable conflicts."[111]

The Journalism Code of Practice by the Fourth Estate (https://fourthestate.org/), in addressing the ethics of a free press, notes the importance of fullness in putting content into the public domain: "Do not omit facts that are material to an understanding of what you are reporting on." As they put it: "There is bad opinion writing and good opinion writing."[112]

Many local Bay Area media are on the same page.

For example, the *San Francisco Chronicle* has a Conflicts of Interest Policy that provides: "We will inform the public about important issues and events in a manner that is upfront, transparent and professional. In doing this work, we must avoid conflicts of interest, both real and perceived, that could affect our audience's perception of the fairness, truth and accuracy of our news coverage."[113]

The Bay Area News Group, of which the *San Jose Mercury News*, *East Bay Times*, and *Marin Independent Journal* are members, has an Ethics Policy that reflects an avowed commitment "to the highest ethical standards. Fairness and accuracy are among our core values. But nothing stands above the need to maintain our integrity. The public's trust—our most important asset—depends on it."[114]

The Press Democrat, on the other hand, does not seem to have any articulated code of ethics, at least not one publicly posted. No surprise perhaps that when it came to the financial entanglement of some of its owners and the SMART project, it said nothing about the conflict until local citizens publicly called the paper out. And when they did, *The Press Democrat* grabbed a shovel and dug a deeper hole.

The paper responded to concerns about its undisclosed conflict in a February 20, 2020, editorial.[115] It could easily have tendered a professional version of "my bad," confessing to the omission with regret while holding tight to the genuineness of its editorial viewpoints. It did not, however. It went on the offensive, branding the temerity of anyone challenging their handling of the conflict as "scurrilous," raising suspicions higher and compounding the problem. It also professed its unassailable objectivity.[116]

"In 1990, the paper endorsed Measure B, a proposed sales tax to widen Highway 101 and start a rail transit system in Sonoma County. Measure B failed, but our support for North Bay rail has continued, with more than two dozen editorials appearing between 1990 and 2012."[117] It then quoted from editorials in 2001, 2006, and 2011 to show it had supported SMART before Anderson and Bosco became its owners, implying that its historical consistency belied any bias in coverage.[118]

And, albeit post facto and sans the juicy details, it begrudgingly made a form of disclosure about Anderson and Platinum Advisors:

> For the record, Darius Anderson isn't a member of our editorial board, and neither are any of the investors named in the anti-SMART flier. None of them has ever tried to influence our positions. They see our editorials at the same time you do—when they appear in *The Press Democrat*.

> As for Anderson's connections to SMART, he owns Platinum Advisors, a lobbying company in Sacramento. One of his employees represents transit agencies, including SMART, and helped secure federal funding to extend service to Larkspur and qualify SMART for a share of revenue from Regional Measure 3, a Bay Area bridge toll increase approved by voters in 2018.[119]

That day, when the editorial ran, Platinum Advisors terminated its lobbying contract with SMART.

It should also be noted that, in the February 2020 editorial, the editorial board, kind of, copped to its omission:

> Some readers say we could have avoided any controversy by including that information in our Feb. 2 editorial ("Yes on Measure I: Don't derail SMART train"). They're probably right.[120]

Probably?

It also missed the point in a few respects.

First, an assessment of the underlying conflict should focus not only on whether *Press Democrat* owners with financial stakes in the covered subject matter leaned into editorial content, as bad as that would be, but also whether the paper came clean with the public in advance with a proper disclosure.

Second, conflicted-ownership top-down editorial control is not the only vice. The existence of conflict can affect judgment, whether as a factor a board overtly considers in deciding what to include in an editorial or, as can easily be the case, through unexpressed and conscious influence. That is why so many newspapers have well-considered and expressed ethics policies, to raise consciousness and provide a reminder and a buffer against slipping into forbidden bias.

Third, scrutiny of the underlying conflict should examine not only whether its support for SMART enjoyed historical consistency, but also the manner in which it expressed that support. Consider some examples of selective editorial support since ownership changed hands in 2016.

In the same February 20, 2020 editorial, in recommending a yes vote on Measure I, the failed measure that attempted to extend the sales tax collection period by thirty years, *The Press Democratic* editorial board cavalierly dismissed SMART's core failing. "Yes, there still is traffic on Highway 101 at rush hour," without addressing the data showing SMART had not made a dent in traffic congestion, the sine qua non of its existence, and that for all the hullabaloo, the rail system had not (and most likely would never) reduce traffic congestion during rush hours on Highway 101.

That same superficiality appeared in its subsequent July 2020 editorial. "When people ride transit, it means fewer vehicles on the road, less congestion, less pollution and safer travel."[121] Again, the contrary data be damned, including the reality that if the commuter rail does not reduce traffic, the diesel fumes from its trains, plus gas fumes from cars getting to its stations, add to air pollution.

"Yes, you can find a seat on most SMART trains,"[122] without acknowledging that SMART's ridership numbers were woefully low by any recognized measure and that its train cars were often virtually empty; or as Dick Spotswood, a former Marin County elected official and current politics and government columnist for the *Marin Independent Journal* recently put it, "when people look through the train's picture windows, they often see empty seats,"[123] words you won't hear from *The Press Democrat*.

"Yes, fares are subsidized,"[124] again ignoring data showing that SMART rider subsidies—measured with farebox recovery—compares grimly with other commuter rail systems.

It was as if the paper said, "we probably should mention these items in passing, but better we scratch the surface for fear of casting the program in a negative light," at a time, it must be stressed, SMART was asking taxpayers to shell out money for an additional *thirty years*.

But the major omission, the one that spoke volumes about how they approached the conflict of interest, was how the editorial board handled the 2018 legislation and the surrounding circumstances that entangled SMART, NCRA, NWP, Platinum Advisors, and its owners, Messrs. Anderson and Bosco.

Recall that the legislation led to SMART acquiring part of the freight business, a major addition and departure from their initial mission as a passenger rail system. As a material change in SMART's future, it raised all sorts of questions worthy of public debate. For example, was SMART an unwitting shill for putting dollars in NWP's pockets? Did the SMART board fail to do adequate diligence in assessing the financial bona fides of expanding its operations to freight, as one board member argued? Was it fair and proper to expect taxpayers, who SMART, *The Press Democrat*, and others sold on a *passenger rail* system, to subsidize a *freight* system too?

And with the SMART freight business operating consistently at a loss—according to *Marin Independent Journal*,[125] SMART reported recently "a $573,000 shortfall in its freight budget for the 2023–2024 fiscal year"—shouldn't SMART have been called out for wasting taxpayer dollars, harkening to an August 2011 *Press Democratic* editorial that called upon SMART leadership to assure taxpayers know that "every tax dollar is being spent wisely"?[126]

And what about all the financial conflicts?

Regardless of the ultimate conclusions, each question deserved incisive editorial scrutiny.

So, when that complex web of relationships, money flow, conflicts of interest, and SMART entanglement bled into the public domain, what did the editorial board of *The Press Democrat* have to say?

Nothing.

The Press Democrat editorial board uttered not a word.

How come?

Did the editorial board decide to turn collective blind eyes to what happened here—and abandon the public trust—because its owners were head deep in the entire imbroglio? Why didn't the editorial board unravel that web of transactions, exposing the conflicts and the wheeling and dealing, and scrutinizing the "wisdom" of SMART to jump into the freight business? SMART stepped into the shoes of NCRA and assumed responsibility for providing freight service from Healdsburg to the Sonoma-Mendocino County line. Why wasn't that an affront to taxpayers doling out hard-earned monies for a commuter rail line—and not a freight operation—and thus a topic primed for editorial commentary? Why didn't *The Press Democrat* editorial board jump all over that and champion the interests of its taxpaying readership?

After waving the SMART flag for more than a decade, was it all too hot a potato to handle for fear of top-down reproach and repercussions?

In a June 28, 2023, editorial, *The Press Democrat* editorial board took US Supreme Court Associate Justices Sam Alito and Clarence Thomas to task for not disclosing gifts they'd received, complaining about their lack of transparency and failure to publicly acknowledge at least the perception of a conflict of interest: "Who their friends are is not the issue.

Rather, it's that they aren't transparent about their gifts and don't step aside when the public reasonably perceives a conflict." The board also urged the High Court to heed national calls for ethical reform: "Justices should heed those calls and impose clear ethical rules about disclosure and conflict of interest on themselves."[127]

Fair points and well said. Perhaps *The Press Democrat* should take a long pull from the same chalice of brewed advice it offered the High Court justices in Washington, D.C.

It is easy to underestimate the subconscious impact of a conflict. It is one thing to say in a candid and well-intentioned way that an editorial is unbiased despite a lurking conflict. It is quite another not to recognize the subtle capacity of a conflict to influence judgment. Concealing the conflict undermines trust and calls into question commitment to ethical behavior. Offering readers a point of view that could impact the fiscal interests of those who you pay your salary or to whom you must answer in the chain of command, at the least, warrants disclosure.

The fact that, when called out on the conflict, *The Press Democrat* acted so selectively, defensively, and aggressively, is troubling. It was as if the paper pushed back with, "How dare you question our ethics?"

The less than humble reaction raised the inference that the editorial board feared the disclosure of the financial ties and entanglements of its owners might breed skepticism about the bona fides of its allegiance to SMART. Otherwise, why not add a sentence to any editorials that potentially implicated the financial interest of its owners? And why not publicly dissect the entangled circumstances that spawned the ethical problem? The head-in-the-sand mentality made it fair game for readers to view SMART editorials with a jaundiced eye.

Far from a watchdog, *The Press Democrat* editorial board has shown a pattern, with some narrow exceptions, of unusually favorable treatment of SMART. Interestingly, in July 2016—after Anderson and Bosco acquired ownership of the paper—in lauding SMART and its anticipated (and much delayed) launch of service, *The Press Democrat* closed an editorial this way: "Let's not blow it."[128]

Us?

The import was that the paper did not draw any lines between itself, SMART, and the public; only a single unified team, each with distinct roles to play dedicated to a common mission and pursuing an agreed goal. It raised the question: In its zeal, did *The Press Democrat* not only drink the SMART Kool-Aid but also package and dole it out by the gallons to its loyal and unsuspecting readership?

* * *

On May 1, 2025, Sonoma Media Investments (SMI) sold *The Press Democrat* to MediaNews Group (an Alden Global Capital subsidiary), a media conglomerate, ushering in a new era of corporate nonlocal news reporting and journalism. In announcing the acquisition, Sharon Ryan, a senior executive with MediaNews Group, noted that new ownership would "seek efficiencies in business operations, distribution and production while striving to support and prioritize the robust, local newsgathering needed to serve the communities that rely on Sonoma Media."[129] Other formal announcements struck a similar chord. None spoke of journalistic integrity and the maintenance of ethical standards, perhaps an oversight in the excitement of the moment.

As *The Press Democrat* enters a new chapter under MediaNews Group, the public is entitled to a cautious hope that the new ownership will uphold a stronger commitment to transparency and ethical journalism—free from conflicts of interest—than what was seen under its predecessor. The expectation at least is that the new leadership—despite its corporate lineage—will adopt a more open, principled approach to covering and commenting on the SMART debacle, driven by a journalistic duty of fairness, accuracy, and independence.

5

The Delayed (and Inauspicious) SMART Launch

Life Support on Arrival

The long-awaited launch of the SMART train carrying paying commuters crystallized what had plagued the project from the start: an unapologetic inability to comprehend the difference between a grandiose vision and raw reality.

Delay

First, there was the matter of the protracted delay in getting trains running.

Through Measure Q, SMART secured voter authorization for a quarter-cent sales tax to finance the project in 2008. The

SMART July 2008 Funding Plan identified the "fall of 2014" as the start-up of commuter service. The subsequent 2008 SMART Expenditure Plan that accompanied Measure Q, while less precise, projected a "passenger train start-up in 2014."[130]

In either case, SMART promised voters it would only take six years to launch service and begin generating revenue to support train operations via collection of the approved sales tax.[131] It is not clear whether SMART leadership fully appreciated the complexities of launching a commuter train operation in the circumstances. They were not railroad people. They were politicians who had an agenda formulated in accordance with a vision that they espoused would revamp the concept of local commuter transit. And their handling of the process showed their lack of experience and competence.

The threshold problem, however, the one that would haunt SMART during the ramp-up period causing enormous delay, was the extent to which the project faced the risk of a funding shortfall, a problem that SMART well knew from the start but swept under the rug publicly.

The project description in the Measure Q voter pamphlet placed all bets on collecting the sought-after sales tax, as a direct source of revenue and the backup to repay contemplated construction bonds SMART planned to issue.[132] Opponents of Measure Q jumped on this in the voter pamphlet in arguing against the ballot measure: "Perpetual taxation. The 20-year quarter-cent tax would cover a fraction of costs, and subsidize only 14 years of operation. Additional funds would be needed."[133] Measure Q Proponents did not respond to that argument. In fact, Measure Q proponents conspicuously avoided mention of project funding in the voter pamphlet.

SMART was not forgetful or sloppy. They stayed mum on the funding problem for a strategic reason. Their own consultants had concluded in 2005 that a quarter-cent sales tax would not raise enough money to fund construction and train operations for a seventy-mile rail line. SMART could ill afford candor in this regard and expect Measure Q to pass. Transparency about inadequate funding would kill the measure. Better to shield it from the public eye as much as possible. In fact, in putting Measure Q on the 2008 ballot, as well as with similar earlier measures, SMART proponents wanted to ask the public to authorize *a half a cent* sales tax rather than *a quarter cent*. SMART knew that for the project to work as envisioned it would require revenues that only a half percent sales tax could generate. But an advance voter poll showed that requesting the larger amount would be the death knell of the measure. The public did not have the appetite for that great a sales tax for the rail line. So, SMART deployed a version of bait and switch, baiting for funds it knew would not do the trick and switching to another unknown funding plan later. SMART had rolled the dice on the backs of local taxpayers.

Later, in 2014, the Sonoma County Grand Jury called them on it, faulting SMART directors for their failure to inform voters about the known risks to its tax revenue projections.[134]

Out of the box, in investment parlance, SMART, to put it mildly, was thinly capitalized and on a balance sheet test, bankrupt. A cynic might think the SMART board rationalized things this way: "Once we have the public on the hook for the tax, it would be politically untenable for government funding sources, whether regional, state, and federal, not to step into the breech and save the day to avoid leaving the public hanging out there."

The funding shortfall was bad enough. Worse, it meant SMART had no margin for error should something occur in the near future to adversely impact their financial situation. And lo and behold, that is precisely what happened, or at least, that is what SMART claimed happened. According to SMART, the national economic downturn in 2008–2009 drove down sales tax revenues, raising a serious question of whether SMART had the financial wherewithal to issue construction bonds to build needed infrastructure for the seventy-mile rail line. Whether that is why SMART was shortchanged—the economy was already in meltdown at the time of Measure Q—remains an open question. Apart from the fact that SMART never provided evidence or a study to support such a claim, it ignored the debt service side of its balance sheet and how interest rates had *declined* between 2008 and 2012 (when the bonds were issued), saving SMART millions of dollars of debt service and its failure to account for changes in wages for construction workers. One thing is for sure: it seems SMART used the recession to cry wolf and divert attention from its lack of initial financial readiness, including the many cost miscalculations in its financial projections and the Measure Q lie that the sale tax revenues were virtually all it needed to finance the project.

Despite the looming financial crisis, in its 2010 Annual Report, SMART waxed optimistic:

> During FY 2009–2010, SMART has met key milestones as the agency has completed the Advanced Conceptual Engineering phase of the project, setting the stage for preliminary and final engineering and construction packaging strategies as we move toward construction activity in 2011 and 2012. . . . Collection of Measure Q sales taxes began April 1, 2009, and in late June 2009, SMART received its first payment of Measure Q sales tax revenue. In the ensuing year, Measure Q generated about $25 million for the project, providing funding to move the passenger train and pathway project forward to its opening in Fall 2014.[135]

Others, however, casting a more objective eye, saw things differently.

For example, in 2010, the Marin County Grand Jury urged SMART to postpone the $91 million bicycle and pedestrian pathway originally allocated under Measure Q to help ameliorate the serious financial shortfall in available funds that jeopardized the then-schedule for starting up the train.[136]

In June of that year, *The Press Democrat* reported that SMART consultants were scrambling to update "construction estimates, looking for cost-cutting measures and revising tax revenue projections."[137] And in November of that year, *The Press Democrat* noted that:

> Rising construction costs and sinking sales tax revenue have left Sonoma-Marin Area Rail Transit with a $350 million gap between how much it has and what it will take to build a 70-mile line by 2014. *The financial report is a stunning blow to the agency, which had promised voters two years ago that passing a quarter-cent sales tax increase would be enough to get the 70-mile commute line running by 2014.*[138] (Emphasis added.)

The alarming situation caused some local politicians to call for a time-out. As reported in *The Press Democrat*, one local politician urged SMART "to defer its start-up plans until the plan and sales tax projections are subjected to an outside review."[139]

SMART would have none of that. It intended to forge ahead, despite the lack of necessary funds. Its response was to revamp rollout plans by building the commuter rail *in segments*, implying that service would be delayed to some communities until well beyond 2014, which nonetheless remained the target date of service commencement.

Sure enough, *The Press Democrat* reported in April 2011: "Hard hit by a recession that has depressed revenues from a quarter-cent sales tax, SMART has been forced to scale back its plans to build a 70-mile commuter line from Larkspur to Cloverdale by 2014."[140] SMART eventually reported that it intended to have trains up and running between Santa Rosa and San Rafael by 2015, about forty miles of track in all. It would worry about the balance of the promised seventy-mile track down the road.

It seemed a work hardly in progress.

In July 2011, *The Press Democrat* noted:

> Sonoma-Marin Area Rail Transit officials will release new financial figures Friday that may cause a redesign of the plan and possibly delay the start of service between downtown Santa Rosa and downtown San Rafael. . . . To meet . . . cost projections, the SMART board identified $88 million in cost-saving measures. It is also counting on receiving $10 million from the [Metropolitan Transportation Commission] (MTC), $8 million from the Transportation Authority of Marin and $3 million from the Sonoma County Transportation Authority. . . . To receive those funds, however, the MTC is requiring SMART to submit a report by July 27 re-affirming that costs have not risen beyond earlier estimates, or it will trigger new hearings and discussions. . . . [SMART Chairwoman Valerie] Brown acknowledged that failure to meet MTC conditions for funding would be a setback for SMART. She also acknowledged that a delay is something the SMART board will have to consider. "I think it is something the board will be looking at," Brown said. "With every month we move down the line it causes concern. Whether to delay or not: does it mean two months or four months? There are a lot of iterations of what a delay will mean."[141]

Despite securing funds from MTC and completing the sale of $191 million in construction bonds to start upgrading and installing new track on the first segment of the rail line, the future remained shrouded in uncertainty. And in December 2013, SMART announced the prospects of a *three-year delay*. As *The Press Democrat* reported, SMART general manager Farhad Mansourian stated: "Our goal is to make sure we are up and running by Christmas 2016. . . . If it's the first half of 2016, I'm going to surprise everyone, but I don't want to get pinned down to that simply because there are many moving wheels."[142]

One way SMART found to ameliorate the financial stress was to jack up fares. In July 2016, the SMART board voted (9–2) to charge up to $9.50 for a one-way trip from Santa Rosa to San Rafael, or $19 round-trip. Future commuters were not happy, as *The Press Democrat* reported: "Rail officials have faced considerable backlash from North Bay residents concerned the fares are too high. The decision, critics say, came with little public input. "'Clearly, we made a number of people very unhappy,'" said Jake Mackenzie, a SMART director and vice mayor of Rohnert Park who voted with the board majority.[143]

The Press Democrat noted further that: "critics say the fares are too expensive and won't entice the North Bay commuters who drive solo—SMART's primary targeted customer base. Some also argue the charges are an affront to the financial sacrifices taxpayers in the two counties have made, and will continue to make, through the quarter-cent sales tax that supports the rail line through at least 2029."

"'We failed miserably," said SMART director Shirlee Zane, who joined fellow Sonoma County Supervisor David Rabbitt in voting against the approved fares. "What we've done, in effect—and I want to be clear, I didn't vote for this—by approving these very high fares, the public has said,

'We've been paying for this train for eight years. It's public transportation, and now you're going to turn around and charge us these really outrageous fares?'"[144]

The summer of 2016 brought another problem, this one seemingly beyond SMART's control. A Toronto commuter train system experienced a major failure with one of its engines, the same diesel model SMART planned to use, and the only other system using that diesel engine, requiring a massive replacement undertaking that included extensive safety testing. SMART general manager Farhad Mansourian advised the SMART board in an October 2016 memo: "This new engine problem, and the need to complete our system-wide safety testing . . . has led me to the conclusion that beginning of passenger service by the end of 2016 is not advisable. We will be working even harder and target late spring 2017 as our beginning of passenger rail service."[145]

So by the end of 2016, SMART had yet to transport a single passenger, and while the latest problem could not fairly be dropped at SMART's doorstep, the vibe remained negative. As the *Pacific Sun* noted in March 2017: "Even the most ardent supporter of a commuter train linking Sonoma County to central Marin County has to be feeling a little skeptical these days."[146]

The start-up of service date had become a slippery slope, with the latest projected date "late spring" 2017, while massive costs continued to pile up. According to its audited financials, SMART had spent about *$600 million* without transporting a single paying passenger. In the world of venture capital and start-up companies, it would be the antithesis of investment models. But unlike the venture capital world, this was not SMART's money to lose. SMART was leveraging "other people's money."

Darius Anderson speaks for Kings investors at a Sacramento City Council meeting in March 2013. (Newscom)

Deb Fudge, former councilmember and mayor, Town of Windsor. Former board member and chair, SMART. (Crista Jeremiason, *The Press Democrat*)

Supervisor Chris Coursey. (John Burgess, *The Press Democrat*)

SMART general manager Farhad Mansourian sits down for a Q&A at the SMART headquarters in Petaluma on Friday, August 18, 2017. (Christopher Chung, *The Press Democrat*)

Eddy Cumins, general manager of SMART, Thursday, December 9, 2021 in Santa Rosa. (Kent Porter, *The Press Democrat*)

Marin County Supervisor Judy Arnold, who represents the Novato area, was elected in 2006 and reelected in 2010 and 2014. (Photo by Frankie Frost/2016, *Marin Independent Journal*)

Senator Mike McGuire, President pro Tempore of the California state senate. (State of California, public domain, via Wikimedia Commons)

Senator Bill Dodd listens to a speaker during a town hall meeting called "Seeking Solutions: A Community Policing Forum" at Vallejo High School, in Vallejo, California, on Saturday, September 7, 2019. (*San Francisco Chronicle*/Hearst Newspapers via Getty Images)

Mike Arnold, economist, stands for a photo in San Rafael, California on November 15, 2016. (MediaNews Group, *Marin Independent Journal* via Getty Images)

Lawyer, former US representative, and businessman Doug Bosco.

Molly Flater, Donor for the Not So SMART campaign.

Komron Shahhosseini, Gallaher family advisor.

Cindy Gallaher

Bill Gallaher

Rep. Jared Huffman (D-San Rafael) represents California's second district. (US Government, public domain, via Wikimedia Commons)

SMART train service begins on the North Coast. (Photo by George Rose)

Despite the setbacks, the SMART people continued to trumpet optimism. For example, Daniel Hillmer, who represented Marin County mayors and councilmembers on the SMART board, asserted that SMART "is on schedule," an assertion that boggled the mind, and that "SMART is performing according to the Measure Q requirements," another assertion that rang hollow. The truth was that Measure Q, then eight years old, promised voters a fully operational train from Cloverdale to Larkspur by 2014, financed with a quarter-cent sales tax. It had broken that promise.

In June 2016, the start-up date continued to evade. SMART general manager Farhad Mansourian put the blame on the Federal Railroad Administration, which had not completed its full audit of SMART's operations and had yet to approve SMART's "Positive Train Control" system that prevents derailments. Nonetheless, Mansourian promised service would start "in the very near future."

In July 2017, the *San Francisco Chronicle*, in commenting on the long delay of the SMART start-up of service, said, "when shovels hit the ground a little more than three years [after voters approved the sales tax in 2008] in a ceremony in Petaluma, no one anticipated it would take quite this long to turn tax dollars into transit service." But SMART evidently assured the newspaper that not only were they "close to opening but [were] moving to build out a network that could have profound impact on the region's residents, its job centers and its growing tourism." In addition, the *Chronicle* reported that the train link to Larkspur would not occur before "early 2019." The paper also noted, "How popular the service will be remains a nagging question."[147]

The start-up of service finally arrived in late August 2017. When it was ready to roll, SMART flooded the market with promotional materials, earmarking August 25, 2017, as the birthdate of its commuter service. Its chief public cheerleader, *The Press Democrat*, published about twenty articles in August and September 2017 rallying around the project. As the paper reported, Debra Fudge, chair of the SMART board proclaimed: "'We are just beyond excited. It's the beginning of a new era of transportation for the whole North Bay, [a] generational change for travel between two counties. It's a red-letter day.'"[148]

Hardly red letter. As Dick Spotswood, a Marin *Independent Journal* columnist noted in his August 14, 2018 column: "SMART bears the negative fruits of rail proponents who oversold the concept in the 2008 election. . . . The sales tax to fund the full 70-mile line as promised should have been a half-cent, not a quarter-cent. That's why the line won't get past Windsor until the late 2020s and its finances are perpetually tight."[149]

The results of the train service launch were, in reality, notably less momentous than how they were touted. On the contrary, they foretold a dubious future.

Demographics Served

SMART envisioned a commuter base that would qualify as a veritable melting pot of local residents. Here is what it said in its first White Paper of 2008: "Who will ride SMART? Students headed to Dominican University or Santa Rosa Junior College, tech workers at Autodesk in San Rafael, insurance adjusters at Fireman's Fund in Novato, clerks and probation officers working at county offices in Santa Rosa, planners and bailiffs heading for the Civic Center in Marin, lawyers and dishwashers headed to jobs up and down the line. (And those are just the commuters)."[150]

The facts turned out quite differently. Ridership started (and continued to be) predominantly white, with an average rider about forty-six years old living in a household of three and earning just shy of $100,000 a year. A mere 15 percent of riders classified themselves as Hispanic compared with a population of 27 percent in Sonoma County and 16 percent in Marin County.[151]

A realistic and informed view would be that the less affluent, the working-class residents of Marin and Sonoma County, were subsidizing the recreational train rides of the middle class. The promise of an egalitarian and utopian transportation system that would transform how people moved about their daily lives in the modern world got instantly exposed as Pollyannaish.

Ridership

In terms of ridership, here is what SMART told everyone to expect.

SMART initially projected ridership of approximately 5,000 boardings per weekday (2,500 riders), which would increase with higher gas prices to approximately 6,000 trips (3,000 riders) based on $5.00 a gallon pricing, weekend service ridership of approximately 2,000 on Saturdays and 1,200 on Sundays and holidays, and approximately 7,000 to 10,000 people daily on the bicycle/pedestrian pathway.[152] In March 2011, it projected its trains would carry about 2,900 passengers a day when service begins and once service extends to the full seventy miles, as many as 6,550 passengers a day. It also indicated that the "vast majority" of its projected ridership would use the rail line to travel between and within the fourteen stations on the seventy-mile track (and not to other ultimate destinations like San Francisco).[153]

It bears noting that, as *The Press Democrat* reported in July 2015, Sonoma Supervisor and SMART board member David Rabbitt "questioned SMART's ridership assumptions, saying they amount to supposition."[154]

In contrast, a week before SMART began transporting paying commuter passengers, Debra Fudge of the SMART board said: "We're confident that we're going to have very full trains."[155] (The number of SMART trains that have *looked* full so far during its several years of operations can probably be counted on one hand).

But even *The Press Democrat*, peering through its rose-colored lens, noted that same day: "Whether SMART can achieve its goal of carrying 3,000 weekday riders remains to be seen."[156]

Other than on the first anniversary of the start-up of service, SMART has never reached three thousand a day and is currently reporting woefully less.

The first six days of paid operations for SMART saw weekday ridership shy of projections, although weekend traffic exceeded target numbers. According to SMART, roughly 2,500 to 2,900 riders used SMART trains daily from Monday through Thursday of the first week—under *discounted fares* in place through Labor Day—relatively close to the initial projection of three thousand riders on weekdays, when the transit system runs thirty-four trips. The first weekend of operations, meanwhile, saw about two thousand daily passengers. And at the time of the start of commuter service, the bike and pedestrian pathway had not been built.[157]

While SMART proponents praised the results—the *Marin Independent Journal* proclaimed: "The SMART train has answered its critics"—in terms of laying a robust foundation for reducing traffic congestion, the numbers smacked of grim news. SMART had given it their best shot. They used discounted rates. They promoted robustly. They had supporters champing at the bit to ride the train after suffering a painful delay in service. It was a grand opening, the kind that normally brings an overflowing crowd waving flags. In other words, the performance on August 25, 2017 was about as good as SMART could ever expect (as subsequent history would confirm). The launch conditions were ideal. Given what was at stake, and given the increasingly conspicuous long-term limitations, the 2017 launch, despite all champagne-popping self-congratulations, portended a plunge deeper into the red, edging closer and inexorably to ultimate failure.

6

Ridership Reality: The Ghost Train to Nowhere

A cost-effective and feasible public transit systems cannot be designed for any location. The underlying conditions must be ripe for constructing a broadly accessible transit service capable of achieving reasonably stated goals in a cost-efficient manner. It would not, for example, be sensible to install a SMART-like system in Sierra or Alpine counties in California. The transit needs there are too sparse, the locations of commuter destinations too diffuse (and not concentrated), and the populations too slight. Any inclination to invest significant public funds in a rail system for isolated communities like those would be undeniably irrational. The conditions are not suitable and the costs prohibitive. You might as well build a monorail in Springfield.

The SMART train program from the start has—and will always have—suffered a fatal flaw that manifests in two integral ways. First, as a matter of design, no matter what

SMART's avowed goals, socioeconomic conditions in Marin and Sonoma counties limit the SMART *potential* for ever achieving ridership levels that will impact traffic congestion on Highway 101. Second, as a matter of historical performance, the SMART ridership numbers are testament to that bare truth. SMART has had *zero* positive impact on Highway 101 traffic congestion.

Potential

SMART was not designed as a recreational transit option for locals to whimsically enjoy on bright sunny days. Rather, it was designed to help solve a major and universally recognized problem: severe traffic congestion in the North Bay on Highway 101. The chief aim of the SMART program was providing local commuters a viable, reliable, regular public transit alternative to using motor vehicles during Highway 101's weekday peak hours. SMART envisioned a rail line with broad demographic appeal across the two counties that would generate maximum ridership for maximum effect, a transformative contribution to modern-day traffic congestion solutions. In the absence of such an ambitious undertaking, SMART could hardly justify asking taxpayers to shell out over one billion dollars to construct and operate the system.

While SMART is not, as such, a business, to stand any chance of even coming close to meeting such lofty goals, it needed to bring a business mentality to how it designed and operated the program. Simplified, its hoped-for riders constituted its customers, and to achieve success of the kind it touted, it had to deliver a product that could draw a substantial and thriving customer base like any successful business with grand ambitions.

The problem for SMART, however, is that socioeconomic conditions in Sonoma and Marin counties militate against that ever happening. Consider one analogy. Most restaurants fail early because of poor accessibility and a misperceived customer base. If a restaurant is set up at an inconvenient location and targets the wrong customers for the area, it would promptly face an unceremonious exit from the hospitality market. SMART suffers from a similar dynamic.

First, the counties of Sonoma and Marin do not contain a critical mass of residents faced each day with deciding whether to take their car or public transit to areas where a substantial concentration of employment, businesses, and schools are located. Compare it to a place like New York City, which while on a significantly larger scale, typifies how a public transit system can work. The public transportation systems in and around NYC serve millions of people who forgo driving into Manhattan or from and to places within Manhattan with available options through the Metropolitan Transit Authority, Staten Island Railway, New Jersey Transit, Port Authority Trans-Hudson, Long Island Railroad, and Metro North Railroad. Those systems are not designed to meet the needs of any specialized class of people but exist to provide transit options for the larger populace who want feasible access to *where employment and businesses are concentrated* throughout Manhattan.

It might be different for Marin and Sonoma commuters if the rail line was available to commuters headed to San Francisco, where ample employment and business concentration exists. For example, pre-Covid, roughly 70 percent of BART passengers traveled from a suburban station into downtown San Francisco (and now, despite that, BART faces its own fiscal cliff). Fundamentally, Sonoma and Marin lack that kind of density. It is the difference between an urban system (serving a concentrated employment center destination) and a suburban rail system (serving disparately located residents and commuter locations).

Destination accessibility is essential to a cost-effective transit system. Where are the employment centers, public services, schools, and areas of commerce located? The more spread out and unconcentrated they are, the more unlikely the system makes sense, unless money is no object (which often appears to be the SMART mindset).

In a 2011 paper titled "Making the Most of Transit Density, Employment Growth, and Ridership around New Stations," Jed Kolko, then associate director of research at the Public Policy Institute of California, and later Under Secretary of Commerce for Economic Affairs in the Joe Biden administration,[158] identified these factors as essential to generating ridership:

- Transit ridership depends on proximity to transit, *especially workplace proximity*.
- *Employment density* is more strongly associated with transit ridership than residential density is.[159]

Public transit success depends on attracting a critical mass of riders who, when faced with the choice of a suburban rail line or their car, will opt for the train because it is designed to get them to their ultimate destinations more efficiently. SMART knew from the start it would never be able to generate that strong a commuter base. Indeed, it bears repeating that the SMART EIR projected that only 230 Sonoma County residents would take the morning SMART trains into Marin County.

Second, a related problem is the SMART infrastructure. It is a single-track system, which means train frequency is limited. During peak hours, for example, trains don't depart until *ninety minutes* after the prior train departure. This also means that if one train is delayed, the delay incites a domino effect, getting transmitted in both directions. Time and convenience are essential considerations for the peak hour commuter and, when it comes to the SMART train, its entrenched limitations seriously constrict its ability to generate a critical mass of ridership.

The time it takes for someone to drive to and from their destination is the uninterrupted time they spend *in the car*. When it comes to public transit, however, the amount of time starts when the commuter decides to leave home, not when the mode of transit leaves, and ends the moment the commuter arrives at the destination after completing each trip segment. In the SMART world, the travel timeline is riddled with reconnections and delays. In stark contrast to the driving experience, the time it takes for someone to make that same trip on a SMART train is broken into these segments: the initial drive, ride, or walk to the SMART station; the wait for the SMART train to arrive; the trip on the train with all its stops; and the walk or a ride (e.g., a vehicle for hire like an Uber or Lyft or more public transit) with its attendant delay to the final destination. And that duplicates on the return leg home. The inability of commuters to go when they want yields low ridership frequency.

This complaint from a local Sonoma County resident responding to an article on the state of SMART is a testament to the problem: "Nice fantasy. Who is going to ride this thing? I know of no one but let's play the game. Take your car to the parking garage (pay) take the shuttle to the train. Get on the train (pay) go to your get-off point, take a cab/bus/uber to your work (pay). Then to come home, do it all over again. Pay to get back to the train, pay to take the train, take the shuttle back to your car, now you can go home. No thanks, I will take my car."

And that commuter did not even mention all the waiting between each of the steps.

Then there is the first- and last-mile problem, often considered the most important factor in whether commuters choose to use a particular mode of public transit. As noted, the first- and last-mile problem refers to the disconnects between a commuter's points of origin and destination and the locations of transit stations. The first mile covers the distance between the spot where the public transportation leaves the commuter on the first part of the round trip *and* the commuter's ultimate destination, while the last mile covers the distance on the second part of the round trip from the spot where the public transportation leaves the commuter *and* their residence. The entire SMART system is infected with first- and last-mile headaches, which implicates transit accessibility and travel time.

Commuters grappling with first- and last-mile issues often are faced with walking to bridge the gap. In those circumstances, how far the commuter must trek will normally determine whether the transit system is considered accessible. The longer the walk, the less connective and accessible the mode of transportation and, in contrast, the more attractive private car usage. It is commonly accepted that a quarter mile is the *outside* limit of what most commuters will tolerate for last and first miles in choosing or rejecting a particular mode of transportation.

In a July 2020 blog for *Human Transit* titled "Eliminating Public Transit's First-Mile/Last-Mile Problem," transit expert Jarrett Walker wrote: "It begins with a ¼ mile. Most people in the United States are 'comfortable' walking less than a ¼ mile (about 5 minutes for most people) to or from public transit stops. The problem arises when a potential rider is farther than a 'comfortable distance' to the necessary fixed-route stop. Of course, what you define as a 'comfortable distance' may be very different than what I consider to be a 'comfortable distance,' and this distance may vary based on uncontrollable variables such as weather and time of day."[160]

The SMART Larkspur station is a case in point. It is about a quarter-mile walk from the SMART drop-off to the Larkspur Ferry, requiring commuters to trek through a major shopping district, over a busy six-lane roadway (Sir Francis Drake) connecting Highways 101 and 580, and through the Larkspur Ferry parking lot. In 2019, the Transportation Authority of Marin commented on this connectivity problem: "The distance between the SMART Larkspur terminal and the ferry terminal may act as a barrier that could adversely impact SMART ridership since currently there are no known plans for public transit between the two terminals."[161]

In the absence of help from public transit agencies, commuters are faced with various ways to address the disconnect: walking, driving (when parking is available), getting picked up or dropped off, biking, private rides (e.g., Lyft or Uber), scooters, a bus, ride-sharing, employer and public supplied micro transit. In all cases, it is a burden.

To help with the problem, public transit systems have two basic options. One is reconstructing the system as a point-to-point commuter line—which does not have a central hub but fans out from destination to destination. That, of course, is not feasible for SMART, a forever fixed-route system with permanent tracks (not built with SMART riders in mind but for freight) and predetermined route and schedule. The second is adding "micro-transit" options that effectively combine modes of movement and improve connectivity with, for example, e-scooters, carpool and ride-sharing services, bike rentals, and dockless bicycles.

SMART has toyed with the idea of adding shuttles to its stations but has blamed the 2008–2009 recession for the delay in getting the job done. In 2023, it added a shuttle to improve Sonoma County airport access as part of a pilot program called SMART Connect.[162] SMART has described it this way: "a first and last-mile connection between the SMART Airport Station and the Charles M. Schulz–Sonoma County Airport (STS), and the surrounding business corridor." The "estimated wait time is between 5 and 15 minutes, depending on demand."[163] The service is not free. So far, SMART riders have largely avoided the shuttle, jumping on board only nine times a day.

But use of a shuttle, even if extended to other stations, would be a Band-Aid solution to accessibility and time efficiency. It would not address the last-mile part of the problem, that final leg of the trip at the end of a long workday when commuters get dropped off at the initial SMART station and then walk, drive home, or have someone pick them up. Nor, importantly, would it eliminate the extra time that the last segment imposes. Commuters would still have to wait for a shuttle. And shuttle usage exacerbates the existing stress and anxiety and inconvenience with another on-and-off transit leg during peak hours.

Unlike cars, the SMART train will rarely transport commuters to their ultimate destination. SMART riders will always have the burden of finding their own way for the first and final segments of their trips. In this regard, consider the comments of Jed Kolko in the same Public Policy Institute of California paper: "Transit ridership diminishes rapidly as distances from transit stations increase: one-quarter mile is the limit that most people will walk for most trips [citation omitted]. . . . Data from California illustrate how strongly proximity to transit determines ridership—even more for workplace proximity than for residential proximity."[164]

It boils down to this: (1) Where are riders located?; (2) Where are they going?; (3) How accessible and convenient is the mode of transportation?; and (4) What is the cost of getting them there?

The bottom line is that SMART is a suburban rail system that does not serve a dense employment center where people can walk to work and suffers from significant accessibility problems. It will never generate a level of ridership to make a dent in Highway 101 traffic congestion. It's an indelibly flawed system that will continue to breed financial waste, its *coup de grâce*.

Actual

The engrained limitations in the SMART train design are demonstrated in its ridership statistics. Two early numbers are symbolic.

On July 19, 2017, a Wednesday, about one month before the official kickoff of the rail line in August of that year, SMART held one of its trial runs for which it did not charge riders. It logged 4,108 nonpaying riders. On August 26, 2017, a *Saturday*, the first day of paid service, it generated only 1,932 riders on a "manual count" basis. (The paying fares that SMART could account for were 1,666.)[165]

A free ride brought out local residents. The first paid ride, however, an inaugural event on a Saturday when the greatest number of residents were free (without concerns about timely arrival at work) and could experiment with what the rail line experience might be like, generated a woefully poor showing.

The ensuing results were of a piece.

SMART's average weekday ridership—which *includes* commuters who previously used *public* transportation and *not* motor vehicles *and* commuters who rode the train during *nonpeak* hours—was 2,489 (in Fiscal 2018), 2,420 (Fiscal 2019), 1,934 (Fiscal 2020), 471 (Fiscal 2021), 1207 (Fiscal 2022), and 2,206 (Fiscal 2023).[166] Some is Covid-affected; most, however, is not.

Through mid-2023, after almost six years of service, SMART had exceeded three thousand riders—using manual counts—only twenty-three times, including weekends, which translates to *1 percent of commuter days*. Its highest weekday paid ridership was 3,684 on October 20, 2017, shortly after it started service when it operated on the buzz of freshness.

SMART knows it has a ridership problem. It has been ultrasensitive about the numbers, and for good reason. The numbers are bad, though SMART often plays spin doctor when discussing them, and for a long while, hid the ball entirely. It even stonewalled local media from seeing the data, which *The Press Democrat* disclosed to the public on December 12, 2019:

> How full are its trains each day? SMART has repeatedly declined to release daily and weekly ridership figures that would give the public a better gauge of how successful the North Bay's commuter line has been, showing, for instance, who is riding the train and when they are hopping aboard during the week. Over the past four months, SMART officials have refused to provide *The Press Democrat* with the more detailed ridership data—information that other public transit agencies including BART and Golden Gate Transit routinely share. SMART General Manager Farhad Mansourian rejected the newspaper's latest request last week during an interview after the SMART board's regular

> meeting. He suggested that SMART's short history of operations had not prepared it for the release of such data, which he described as "complicated," partly because of the various ways passengers buy tickets and board trains.[167]

And when SMART did release them, it resorted to sleight of hand. On January 3, 2020, *The Press Democrat* reported:

> The daily ridership figures reveal the train's average weekday passenger totals were previously overstated by [SMART general manager Farhad] Mansourian, who has been at the helm of the agency for eight years. In November, he told the *Marin Independent Journal* that on average the system carries about 2,800 riders each weekday. But the agency's figures show it averaged roughly 2,300 passengers on weekdays during its first two years of service, according to a *Press Democrat* analysis of the data. . . . That discrepancy in figures amounts to a difference of more than 94,000 passengers each year, or nearly a sixth of SMART's annual ridership.[168]

A pattern exists. What you see is what you will get. The socioeconomic conditions do not exist in the communities SMART has endeavored to serve to expect any noteworthy change. SMART will forever languish below or around three thousand riders per weekday, for both peak and nonpeak periods. SMART trains average less than 20 percent capacity–just seventy passengers per train.[169]

What does it all amount to in the larger scheme of things? According to Caltrans Ramp Volume reports, there are at least 1.5 million daily vehicle trips on Highway 101 between Airport Blvd (near SMART's northern terminus) and Sir Francis Drake Blvd[170] (SMART's southern terminus after completing the Larkspur extension). Even if ridership reached a consistent three thousand riders per weekday, its train ridership represents a whopping .002 percent of total vehicle trips, *less than 1 percent*. The impact on traffic is, charitably put, negligible and, more candidly, zero, a benefit famine for which taxpayers have doled out *over one billion dollars*. In reality, the percentage is even lower. As noted, the SMART ridership numbers include riders who previously used other forms of *public* transit and thus did not drive their cars, and riders who used the train during *off-peak* hours and thus do not represent any impact on traffic congestion. They also include "replacement" commuters, part of the "substitution effect," car drivers who had earlier opted to go at off-peak hours to beat traffic and who with the onset of SMART replaced SMART riders who had moved from driving to taking the train. Taking those classes of commuters out of the equation plummets the SMART impact even deeper below insignificant, underscoring that SMART has had (and will continue to have) *zero impact* on Highway 101 traffic congestion.

This harkens to what the SMART EIR candidly observed in assessing traffic congestion impact: "Much of the traffic congestion relief would be found on surface streets paralleling Highway 101, rather than on the freeway itself."[171] You will never find that conclusion in any of the SMART voter materials. On the contrary. Running roughshod over its own EIR, SMART made these reckless claims in urging taxpayers to vote for failed Measure R in 2006:

> SMART *provides an alternative to Highway 101 gridlock*, removing 5,300 car trips from our roads during the worst commute hours, more than 1.4 million annually. SMART can be running in 3 years, faster than widening the

> freeway. . . . SMART will remove up to 1.4 million car trips annually from Marin and Sonoma roads during the heaviest traffic times." (Emphasis added.) They said the same thing in urging approval of Measure Q in 2008.[172]

The SMART rail line is littered with false, broken, and empty promises. SMART has been—and will continue to be—a stunning failure.

7

What Were (and Are) They Thinking?

Sustained success in the for-profit world often requires business diversification, a prudent and even visionary strategy to reduce risk and rechart a stronger path forward. Corporate enterprises can ill afford to stand firm. When a business is underperforming or stagnant, market expansion can be just what the corporate doctor ordered.

That mindset, however, is ill-fitting for nonprofit entities operating pursuant to a legislative mandate that taxpayers are financing with an expectation about how their hard-earned tax dollars will be spent. In that circumstance, diverting from the main tracks to chart new ways to generate income can foretell that something may be "rotten in the state of Denmark."

As recounted earlier, in May 2020, SMART acquired the freight assets of NWP Co., a private freight company, with $6 million in gifted state funds, the majority for the purchase price and the balance to address a portion of deferred freight maintenance. The SMART board approved this purchase without performing any advance diligence about potential profitability and without any expertise in running a freight rail system, electing, oddly, to assess feasibility afterward. SMART evidently hoped that the freight business would become an independent profit center to shore up their financially poor performing commuter rail system.

SMART and their political backers would never concede that the foray into the freight transportation industry was a cry for help, a glaring red flag, or at the least in hindsight, a seriously misguided undertaking. Bureaucratic and political mindsets tend to avoid such refreshing acknowledgment of errors. But it is painfully obvious that SMART's acquisition of a local freight business has quickly become, if it wasn't from the start, a fool's errand.

SMART exists to advance a straightforward mission: to operate a local public commuter rail system that reduces nearby highway traffic congestion in an environmentally sound manner. Recall the main argument in favor of Measure Q, the sales tax ballot measure taxpayers approved to fund SMART: "Marin and Sonoma County voters can take a positive step . . . to protect the environment, relieve traffic, and provide for our long-term transportation future."[173]

Ridership, however, has underwhelmed and fare recovery has been woeful. Traffic impact never materialized and environmental impact has been flat at best, if not negative.

SMART thought diversifying into the freight business could improve this weak state of affairs. As *The Press Democrat* reported: "SMART officials say expanding into freight rail could diversify the agency's business and boost revenues with a separate income stream tied to shipping bulk goods."[174]

California Senator Mike McGuire, the architect of the freight gambit, waxed philosophical about the prospects, claiming that the takeover of freight operations would allow SMART "to control their own destiny,"[175] classic financial-speak to mask a stagnating business. At least Senator McGuire got the destiny part right, just not how he envisioned.

Even the SMART-friendly *Press Democrat* wondered about the wisdom of this great leap forward: "The North Bay's passenger rail system is moving into freight operations, and one of the governing board's first decisions about the scope of those operations is likely to make them a money loser, at least at the outset."[176]

NWP Co. had four freight customers—grain to Lagunitas Brewing and three livestock feed companies—and stored freight cars for five entities to generate leasing revenue, a sizable chunk of its total revenue. Doug Bosco, a former congressman and part owner of *The Press Democrat*, and a recipient of the sale of the business, forewarned: "[SMART will] be working pretty hard to get (revenues) up to where they are now."[177]

SMART was undaunted.

"SMART directors have said they are confident the agency can find customers to make freight rail pay, and have argued consolidated control over the North Bay's rail lines will be a public benefit."[178]

The avowed confidence came on the heels of a report SMART issued in December 2021 on its new freight business. Among other things, the report forecast freight revenues, although it did not include anything similar for expenses. The forecasts, set out in a visualization data chart, predicted total operating revenues for what SMART called "a divergence of revenue outcomes over the next 10 years [through 2030], primarily dependent upon how SMART elects to manage its freight operations." It posited three scenarios: "Downside," "Base Case," and "Upside."[179]

The "Downside" Scenario.

Even before setting forth the forecasts, SMART dismissed the importance of the "Downside" scenario: "The Downside scenario is not intended to be a forecast of future events—only an illustration of the impact that various possible outcomes could potentially have upon freight traffic and revenue levels."[180] It was as if SMART said, "Don't pay much mind to the Downside scenario and let's ignore what can go wrong. It's included only to demonstrate our diligence." Keep that in mind when looking at the actual numbers (below).

The "Downside" forecast showed annual operational revenues starting at $1,200,000, declining to $1,000,000 by 2022, dipping slightly the next two years, and flattening the remainder of the forecasted ten-year period at $1,000,000.[181]

The "Base Case" Scenario.

Here is SMART on this scenario: "This forecast assumes that the freight service continues to function as it has in recent years, with essentially the same operating and 25 commercial practices. This is essentially a 'status-quo' forecast without any significant changes or major investments by SMART."[182]

Consider how Senator Mike McGuire described that same status quo:

> [NWP Co] was a hot mess. They were in massive debt, teetering on bankruptcy and had completely failed their mission over the last 20 years to provide freight rail to the North Coast. They should have been shut down years ago.[183]

Not a ringing endorsement.

Bernard Meyers, a Marin County supervisor appointed to the board of the North Coast Railroad Agency (NCRA), which leased freight operations to NWP Co, explained the hot mess shortly after SMART entered the fray:

> What do you call a State agency with a lopsided 105-year lease of a California railroad right-of-way, consummated by way of a series of Brown Act violations and other improprieties, combined with two bankruptcies book-ending the expenditure of nearly $80 million of taxpayer funds, a California Supreme Court decision resulting in the loss of millions of taxpayer dollars, a federal loan application by a public agency that its own Board was forbidden to see, and egregious "no-bid" contracts that cost the public far more than the initial bid amounts?
>
> The answer is the North Coast Railroad Authority.[184]

Onto that battlefield marched an ill-prepared SMART.

Against the backdrop of that tumultuous history and rocky under footing, SMART nonetheless forecast the annual "Base Case" revenue starting at about $1,200,000, rising to $1,500,000 million by 2022, rising further to $1,600,000 by 2023, and gradually climbing from there to peak at "nearly" $2,000,000 by 2030.[185]

The "Upside" Scenario.

Here, the forecast "assume[d that] multiple policies favorable to freight development occur in the future," including various financial lifelines, e.g., "rate reductions," "grant funds," and other SMART funds—sounds like local sale tax revenues—to "subsidize freight by limiting fees for use of trackage."

The "Upside" scenario forecasted annual revenues starting at $1,750,000, rising to $1,800,000 by 2022 and $2,000,000 by 2023, and climbing until hitting $2,500,000 in 2030.[186]

Now back to reality.

In December 2022, SMART disclosed freight operational revenues of a mere $547,641, which included $242,789 in "interest and lease earnings," and only $289,395 from "freight traffic." SMART had, it bears noting, budgeted $1,100,000 in "freight traffic" revenues.[187] SMART had expenditures of $402,056 that year, *more than two-thirds* of what SMART generated from freight operations.[188]

In December 2023, SMART disclosed freight operation revenues of only $504,396, $206,852 from "freight traffic" and $46,964 from "interest and lease earnings." They had budgeted $1,004,800 in "freight traffic" revenues. They also disclosed expenditures of $1,059,843, meaning that total revenues, including "miscellaneous" and "interest and lease earnings," are running at *48 percent of expenses* and *freight traffic* revenues are running at *less than 20 percent of expenses*.[189]

Consistent with its internal numbers, SMART reported in March 2023 it would suffer a $573,000 shortfall in its freight budget for the 2023–2024 fiscal year (July 1, 2023 to June 30, 2024).[190]

Perhaps SMART should have added a fourth scenario to their forecasts: the Uber-Downside.

SMART has followed in lockstep with the "hot mess" footsteps of NCRA, demonstrating that its entry into the freight train business was borderline reckless. Sure, controlling the tracks for both commuter and freight transportation might avoid some scheduling conflicts. But that is hardly a responsible basis to acquire a freight transportation business. Beyond that, it has been a big zero. SMART seemed to think that a *local* freight train transportation could be cost-efficient and pull trucks off the local highways. The reality is the opposite. While the train is the environmentally sounder mode of transportation, trucking is otherwise vastly superior over short distances carrying relatively small loads—the SMART freight market—in contrast to the national freight market with its attendant long hauls of substantial loads. Trucks are loaded and unloaded faster than trains, are more dependable in terms of scheduling, have greater flexibility of route if preferred route hazards occur, and, vitally, offer destination to destination service (while trains require an intermodal transportation over the last mile or so, i.e., by truck).[191]

And it will likely get worse.

So far, SMART has apparently not dipped into Measure Q sales tax monies to subsidize its failed freight business. But that can quickly change if the freight operation continues its deep deficits. When the state monies earmarked for the freight operations run out, and revenues cannot keep the freight business afloat, SMART will have to dip its hands into the sales tax coffers. And bear in mind that NWP Co. was a common carrier under federal law and now SMART is. That means SMART is obligated to continue providing freight services no matter how poorly the business is performing—until the federal government puts it out of its misery.

SMART general manager Eddy Cumins recently acknowledged to the SMART board that the freight business "has an operating deficit, it's not subsidized by Measure Q, and it needs to stand on its own," and while SMART has tried to generate new freight customers, that's no small feat for a small market freight business sharing as a single-track with the first fiddle commuter rail system, "it is very difficult to build a business."[192]

***

A separate but related problem plagues the SMART freight business: whether as a revenue source, it should lease storage space on some of its tracks to tankers containing the hazardous Liquid Petroleum Gas ("LPG").

Before SMART dove blindfolded into the freight transportation business, as discussed, NWP Co raised revenue by allowing freight operators to store petroleum tanker cars on its train tracks in southern Sonoma County at the Schellville yard. However, residents in Sonoma, as well as SMART board members, were not happy with the arrangement, not because the revenue was insufficient, but purportedly because constituents lobbied hard about public safety and environmental hazards associated with LPG. In other words, as SMART would presumably concede, they did not walk away from the storage part of the freight operation because it made business sense or in deference to applicable law; they felt compelled to do so because of the political optics, a desire to appease local residents, at the expense of freight revenue.

As a result, SMART terminated the leasing arrangement, a decision that cost SMART an estimated $500,000 to $750,000 in annual revenue, or roughly 30 percent of the freight revenue. SMART tried to attract other rail operators to store environmentally sound rail cars to replace the lost revenue stream, generating virtually nothing.[193] In the 2022–2023 fiscal year, for example, SMART brought in a paltry $7,500 in freight storage revenue.[194]

SMART GM Cumins lamented, "There is no business there."[195]

Given its tenuous financial operating performance in both the commuter rail and freight markets, SMART has recently raised the specter of reversing course on storing LPG tanker cars. "We have an operating deficit and that's the bottom line," Cumins said. "In order for freight rail to sustain itself long-term under the SMART umbrella, we have to find a way to make revenue."[196] David Rabbitt, a SMART board member, candidly acknowledged: "I do think that we need to look at [the tanker storage revenue stream] from a long-term financial perspective as well and figure out what is our financial plan if we're not going to have storage on the freight side of things and we are going to continue to hemorrhage dollars . . . either we need to go back to the state, look for some subsidy, or even locally, if that's the case."[197]

Cumins dismissed the same safety and environmental concerns that initially persuaded SMART to give up the leasing revenue when it acquired the freight business. He told the board he "is not concerned with the storage and does not see a risk associated with the storage. There is a transportation related risk specifically with derailment during train movement."[198]

Not everyone agrees.

Norman Gilroy lives near the Schellville yard and has championed the cause of protecting the community against hazards associated with storing LPG. He has criticized board members "for prioritizing SMART's revenue over community safety."[199] In response to news that SMART was reconsidering its prior decision about the LPG tankers, on November 11, 2023, he sent a voluminous packet to the SMART board, including a bevy of reports and a September 8, 2023 memo to Eddy Cumins.[200]

In summary, Mr. Gilroy maintained that to exhume the LPG freight storage business SMART would need a new permit and an amendment to the Sonoma County General Plan, conduct an Environment Impact Report, install a host of safety improvements, and outlay significant capital expenditures, all at a cost, in his estimate, in excess of $20 million, on top of a delay of about three years.[201] The extent to which that argument is well-founded—the permit requirement, for example, seems misplaced—it highlights the complexity of SMART altering course and jumping back into the LPG tanker storage business.

Comparing that investment to potential annual revenues from anticipated storage leasing contracts, Mr. Gilroy concluded it would take "more than forty years to amortize the capital costs and to show a real flow of unencumbered income to the freight system." It was an investment, he further noted, that could be squandered "should a single explosion and a bleve [boiling liquid expanding vapor explosion] occur" at the storage yard.

His more impassioned argument, which won the day when SMART initially decided to give up storing LPG tankers at the Sonoma yard, focused on environment and safety concerns. Foremost, he underscored the inherently dangerous nature of LPG, an asphyxiant gas that can enflame and explode if ignited, causing death and widespread destruction. In apparent response to naysayers, he reminded the board of an incident in March 2023 when an eight-car freight train derailed at the prior site of the stored petroleum tankers, spilling contents all over SMART train tracks. While the loads on board thankfully were not hazardous, the incident raised the specter of an occurrence considerably more inimical to public health and safety and the environment, including nearby marshlands and wildlife.

To drive home his point, Mr. Gilroy stressed the proximity of the Schellville yard to the community and sensitive resources. He posited that if one or more LPG tankers overturned in the same location as those that met such a fate in March 2023, a resulting bleve could destroy or inflict severe damage upon electrical high-tension transmission lines, vital gas distribution lines, a first-responder fire station, and a sanitation plant, some of the key resources that serve 17,500 residents and are located within the blast zone of the tanker yard. He punctuated his argument with the grim fact that the Schellville yard sits virtually on top of two active earthquake faults.

Mr. Gilroy concluded: "The results of a single accident could be lives lost, property burned or damaged, and sensitive habitat destroyed, all within an impact area larger than the storage yard itself."

He added this zinger: "I doubt very much that any members of the SMART board would vote . . . to place a hazardous materials storage yard . . . across the street from their own residence, or near the home of one of their own grown children."[202]

The SMART board prudently retreated, for the moment, wanting more safety information from fire officials and hazardous materials professionals before making any decision whether to reverse course and revert to leasing LPG tankers.[203]

***

SMART is caught between a rock and a hard place. If they reverse their prior decision and go for the money—they haven't so far—it will emblazon in the public eye the depths of their desperation to save the failing commuter rail system and freight business, including their willingness to impose health and safety and environmental risks on the local Sonoma community. If they affirm the status quo, it will likely sound the death knell of the freight business—they have failed to expand its paltry customer base—or raise the disturbing prospect of grabbing Measure Q funds to run freight operations, laying bare their improvident decision-making and, worse, mocking their sacred trust to Measure Q taxpayers. Both paths impose a substantial political penalty. But SMART and their backers only have themselves to blame, trapped as they are inside a web of their own making.

8

SMART Today

Not So Good

On June 16, 2015, Donald John Trump famously kicked off his presidential campaign by taking a momentous ride down an escalator inside his cherished Trump Tower, smiling from ear to ear and waving with self-assured glee to a raucous and enthusiastic crowd. Trump would later triumphantly observe, in a bit of irony that doubtless escaped him: "It looked like the Academy Awards."[204]

But was the audience that cheered him on that day populated with droves of genuine supporters, dyed-in-the-wool incipient charter members of the budding MAGA movement? Or, conversely, was the audience teeming with shills, with no concern for political stripes?

It did not take long for the answer to emerge. As reported, the Trump presidential campaign paid people to fill space at the celebratory rally (like seat fillers at the Academy Awards), and not just any tourist or local pedestrian plucked off the busy streets of midtown Manhattan, but hungry professional actors always ripe for a gig no matter how inglorious.[205]

The bounty? Fifty dollars a pop per actor.

"Trump's team sent an e-mail to a casting agency asking for performers to wear T-shirts and carry signs and help cheer him in support of his announcement." In consequence, the event became "a full-on production, complete with gossip reporters, a Broadway soundtrack, and people waving signs that read, Donald, we need You!!!"[206]

The Trump campaign had employed an increasingly popular if dubious ethical device known as astroturfing, a member of the fake news family. Typically used in political campaigns to conjure the false image of widespread support for a candidate or a legislative measure, astroturfing, an upside-down play on the term "grassroots movement," is designed to create a bandwagon effect, a fake critical mass that cajoles others into thinking they too should jump on board and rally around the cause.[207] From a sheer psychological perspective, the manufactured support provides comfort to others to join the perceived herd, that they too are doing the right thing and can be bona fide members of a popular group.

Shackled with a historically dismal operating performance—reflected in poor ridership numbers—and suffering from a public image that threatens its viability, SMART seems to have succumbed to the intoxicating allure of astroturfing. A June 2023 Marin County Civil Grand Jury report may have lit the fire under SMART that spawned the new political strategy. The grand jury noted:

> Since Marin and Sonoma County voters in 2008 authorized levying the sales tax to finance SMART's construction and operation, the public has invested more than $600 million. Since trains first began operating in 2017, the weekday

> average ridership has rarely exceeded 2,500. Even though SMART's ridership has rebounded after the Covid-19 pandemic, current ridership remains short of expectations. . . .
>
> The Grand Jury has found that SMART is highly dependent on sales tax revenues for its operations. Without those funds SMART will not be able to continue even if it substantially increases the number of riders or obtains additional federal, state, or regional funds from existing programs.
>
> In fact, SMART will likely be forced to discontinue services if Marin and Sonoma county voters do not approve a sales tax extension by the required supermajority in an election before 2029.[208]

It is easy to see how those ominous words could provoke visions of a massive and humiliating dismantling of the proud SMART commuter rail system and the prospects of a failed legacy of unprecedented proportions and, in consequence, send shivers throughout SMART headquarters.

The grand jury urged SMART to focus on its major weakness, low ridership, by "delineating the value SMART brings to the community." It focused SMART on addressing the structural problems that seemingly have kept commuter ridership down, e.g., the first/last mile connection, a lack of public confidence in its management and board, weak service reliability, and, vitally, underscoring the lack of concentration of "residences, retail, and jobs near SMART's stations," which has been and will likely always be a fundamental flaw in the efficacy of the rail system.[209]

It did not, on the other hand, recommend that SMART buy riders or manufacture ridership numbers by monkeying around with fares or redoubling efforts to increase ridership outside its core mission. Instead, it implored SMART to improve ridership demand by finding ways to increase the appeal of the system to the legislatively targeted rider, the regular weekday commuter.[210]

In response, however, SMART used tax dollars to provide riders *outside* the targeted community with free rides, ostensibly to boost its ridership numbers. Unlike typical purveyors of astroturfing stratagem—the Trump campaign, for example, unsurprisingly denied paying actors to show up and fill space—SMART made no bones about their game plan and motives, to their credit displaying a transparency that had eluded the prior administration. The *Marin Independent Journal* reported on the unveiled strategy:

> [SMART], facing lower farebox revenue and grappling with its financial sustainability, has decided to allow youths and seniors to ride trains for free. Beginning in April [2024], passengers younger than 19 and older than 64 will travel at no cost as part of a one-year pilot program aimed at boosting ridership. The program, approved Wednesday, is expected to sunset at the end of June 2025. It will cost about $282,000. SMART officials said getting more people on the train is the best thing it can do to show voters the value of the system. "We need more riders," said Chris Coursey, a SMART board member and Sonoma County Supervisor.[211]

Mr. Coursey was spot on. SMART needs more riders—many, many more, as the Marin County Grand Jury repeatedly stressed in its report. Since launching in 2017, SMART has failed to meet passenger projections. For example, in fiscal year 2023, SMART's daily weekday average ridership was 1,987 (well below its goal of 2,500) and its comparable numbers for the weekend stood at 1,853. In fact, according to SMART, when compared with weekday rides, "weekend trains have about 55% more boardings on Saturdays and 45% more on Sundays," which prompted SMART to add extra weekend trips to stoke the ridership numbers.[212]

In other words, the evidence suggests that SMART has devolved into a recreational, publicly subsidized transit system for weekend enthusiasts as much as it is a weekday commuter system for working people transporting to and from employment destinations (with no meaningful effect, if any, on traffic congestion).[213] To make matters worse, as another gauge of its ridership woes, SMART recently suspended its late-night service after less than five months of operation due to poor usage.[214]

It is likely that SMART will merge ridership numbers in order to eliminate distinctions between riders who pay and those who do not or who pay discounted fares or between weekend recreational riders and weekday commuter riders, allowing it to take cover in gross numbers. Claiming average daily ridership of 3,840, the combination of weekend and weekday riders for fiscal year 2023, as one example, projects a more robust rail system than any candid breakdown of the mathematical pieces that make up the total.

Reenter astroturfing, SMART-style.

As is commonly known, Donald Trump, who may be the patron saint of astroturfing, in his tireless quest to try and outdo former President Barack Obama, went to great lengths to misrepresent the size of the audience that attended his 2017 inauguration. His obedient press secretary Sean Spicer claimed that the inaugural turnout "was the largest audience to ever witness an inauguration, period, both in person and around the globe." When called on it with a series of tell-no-lies photos comparing the inaugurations and showing Trump's turnout was substantially less than Obama's, the Trump minions unabashedly sought cover in a contrived universe they called "alternative facts."[215]

Faced with the realization that a meaningful number of riders cannot come from the natural growth of the weekday commuter rail program, SMART's behavior suggests that they have devised a game plan with a related strategy: Use whatever means available to pump the ridership numbers up to create the false image of operational financial health. That way, SMART can argue all is well, no matter what the "nay-sayers" say, and when the time comes, taxpayers should feel comfortable jumping on board and checking the ballot box to authorize hundreds and hundreds of millions of dollars over thirty years in sales taxes to fund SMART.

In the wake of hatching this new strategy, speaking to the SMART board, GM Eddy Cumins made this admission, giving the back of the hand, perhaps unwittingly, to taxpayers: "We have been intentional that fares are less important than ridership."[216]

Think about that for a second. Fares, the major criterion for determining how much taxpayers are subsidizing the system, are less important than ridership numbers, no matter how they are generated and no matter who fill the seats.

The shift in focus from fares to ridership underscored another problem SMART has had to confront: the farebox revenue recovery ratio metric, which determines the percentage of a transit system's operating costs recovered through passenger fares, the time-honored litmus test for determining transit financial performance.

For more than a decade, SMART has been a proponent of the farebox revenue recovery metric. Indeed, the metric has been a cornerstone of SMART's taxpayer ballot campaigns to persuade locals to tax themselves for the good of the program. For example:

- In its Expenditure Plan for the failed 2006 Measure R, to induce taxpayer support, SMART touted that "Based on the experience of other passenger rail systems, fares are expected to fund approximately 30% of annual rail system operating costs."[217]
- In its Expenditure Plan for the successful 2008 Measure Q ballot, to induce taxpayer support, SMART upped the ante on farebox recovery, claiming that "Based on the experience of other passenger train systems, fares are expected to fund approximately 36% of annual train system operating costs."[218]
- In its Expenditure Plan for the failed 2020 Measure I ballot, SMART elected to stay quiet on farebox revenue recovery for the apparent reason that the actual percentage, after several years of operation and data accumulation, had sunk to 10%.[219]

SMART has good reason to fear the farebox revenue recovery metric. Its ratios have been in steady decline from the start: in 2019, 2020, 2021, and 2022, they were 15 percent, 11 percent, 3 percent, and 5 percent, respectively.[220] And in fiscal year 2023, its farebox revenue recovery was 6 percent, which means that taxpayers are subsidizing 94 percent of operations, a dramatically high number.[221]

For context, regarding farebox revenue recovery, SMART ranks near the bottom of commuter rail systems in the nation and way below the average. And, regarding taxpayer subsidies for commuter rail systems, SMART hits taxpayers up with one of the highest in the nation and, again, way above average.[222]

The appalling state of SMART's financial performance, as measured by the farebox recovery metric, cannot be overstated, which the Marin County Civil Grand Jury felt compelled to address:

> SMART's ridership, and therefore its farebox revenues, declined precipitously during the pandemic and have yet to recover. . . . The end result is that the sales tax has subsidized SMART ridership, ranging from $32 to $75 per ride, with a high of $196 in 2021.[223]

SMART likely knows not only that their historical numbers are bad, but also that providing free rides to improve performance optics will depress the numbers further, which means taxpayers must dole out even more of their money to support the failing operation, a slippery slope into extinction.

The solution: make the standard farebox recovery metric entirely irrelevant.

At the SMART December 20, 2023, board meeting, GM Cumins represented to the board that there is "no right or wrong way" in terms of whether to use farebox revenue recovery to measure financial performance, that "it just depends on what SMART would like to do,"[224] advising the board effectively they have carte blanche to recreate the narrative to improve the public image, national and local standards be damned, and whatever the impact on taxpayers. Indeed, conspicuously absent from the board discussion was any consideration of the impact of abandoning farebox revenue recovery ratios on taxpayers or how, if they abandon that standard metric, taxpayers will know the extent to which they are subsidizing operation of the commuter rail system. The entire board focus was on jacking up the ridership numbers to create an image of healthy financial performance, including through free rides and discounted rates.[225]

A public campaign to advance the new narrative immediately followed. Two days later, SMART board member Chris Coursey stated: "People who oppose SMART and have opposed SMART for years have always latched on to the farebox recovery numbers, but in the end, they don't matter."[226]

Ponder that. Aside from the fact that SMART has used farebox revenue recovery ratios to promote prior ballot measures seeking taxpayer support, a slice of history that perhaps Mr. Coursey forgot, his comment raises this troubling question: Did he mean that "taxpayers" who happen to hold different views than the pro-SMART contingent "don't matter"?

Alternatively, did he mean that *farebox recovery numbers* "don't matter"? That would likely be less offensive to those of his constituents who do not agree with him. But, again putting aside the unflattering lack of familiarity with institutional history, the remark is ill-informed political mumbo jumbo. The notion that farebox revenue recovery ratios for a local commuter rail transit system "don't matter" is absurd and unworthy of crediting.

It is understandable that SMART feels tempted to change the public narrative about how to measure the financial performance of their commuter rail system. But casting aside the approach SMART has long heralded, based on national standards and data, when it suited them as a basis to pry dollars out the hands of local taxpayers, the new narrative looks like a telling sign of desperation.

After advising the board it is acceptable to toss the farebox revenue recovery metric into the dust bin, SMART GM Eddy Cumins tried to fill the metric void another way.

"Cumins said critics focus on the farebox return, or the 'farebox recovery ratio' . . . to measure whether a transit agency is successful. Cumins said a metric called 'investment per passenger mile' provides a clearer picture. The metric is equal to how much the district pays per passenger mile traveled."[227]

Apart from also warranting a failing grade on SMART history, the GM's comments are fairly dubbed political sleight of hand.

First, the national transportation industry uses farebox revenue recovery as a key metric to assess the financial performance of transit systems.[228] So does the local Metropolitan Transportation Commission, the transportation planning, financing, and coordinating agency for the nine-county San Francisco Bay Area.[229] Cumins and the SMART board want to carve out an exception to this well-established custom to advance their political agenda.

Second, the metric Cumins now embraces does not advance the ball the way he would like. In fiscal year 2022, for example, SMART was the fifth most expensive per passenger mile and fifth most expensive per boarding commuter rail system among the thirty-seven commuter rail systems *in the entire nation*.[230] No matter how hard they try, SMART will be unable to make a silk purse out of a sow's ear.

Third, and perhaps most relevant to the public dialogue, the attempt to bury farebox revenue recovery data is an affront to taxpayers. It bears repeating that one major use of the farebox ratio metric for commuter rail systems is informing the public the extent to which *they* are subsidizing the transit operation. It seems SMART not only wants to create a yardstick to manufacture a false positive of financial performance health but wants also to jettison the data that lets taxpayers know what the system is costing *them*. Denying taxpayers that information is an egregious breach of loyalty to taxpayers, unbecoming of stewards of public trust.

We know that taxpayers are subsidizing about 94 percent of SMART operations and we can expect that with the cancellation of fares for certain groups, the number will inch closer to 100 percent. Is the next ploy to let everyone ride for free in the hope that untold members of the community will caravan to SMART stations and pack train cars like a rush-hour New York subway train?

Dependent on more tax dollars to survive, SMART is in deep trouble. It is not surprising its leaders have hunkered down with a bunker mentality in search of ways to justify continued operations. But SMART is not *entitled* to survive. It does not have that privilege. To be sure, in creating the SMART district, the California legislature contemplated the possibility of dissolution (more on that later) by enacting provisions to guide a shutdown of operations.[231]

SMART should only be permitted to survive if it earns that status *on the merits*, in ways that respect the mission and legislative goals of the enterprise that taxpayers have been asked to fund and comport with a dispassionate assessment of costs and intended benefits. Playing around with ridership numbers, revising history, and promoting red herring arguments about how to measure financial performance are disingenuous at best, and at bottom, a tacit admission that SMART has not gotten it done, will likely never get it done, and that time may soon run out.

As the Marin County Civil Grand Jury noted in its June 2023 report: "SMART is at a crossroads—will it be here tomorrow?"[232]

That searing question will be up to Marin and Sonoma county taxpayers to answer.

9

If Things Weren't Bad Enough . . .

In the sphere of macroeconomics, events often intervene that market participants have little or no control over and can be game changers in myriad ways, both positive and negative. External factors that can intrude in that way include the economic, such as a recession; weather, like an earthquake, tornado, or tsunami; technological, such as industry advances that render a product antiquated; and legal, which could be changes in the law that complicate enterprise operations.

These market forces do not often operate in the global theater, but as is well known in recent times, they sometimes do, as the recent pandemic demonstrates, with far-reaching and indiscriminating consequences. Sometimes, businesses are able to adjust and rebound. Other times they fail instantaneously. For others still, the incremental burden from the exterior intrusion can add to an existing amalgam of ills and become the final nail in the coffin.

And so it may be for SMART.

COVID-19 burst onto the international scene, with little or no warning, splattering disorder and destruction across a wide expanse of social, political, and economic terrain. The pandemic did more than cause widespread death and illness, turn lives and families upside down, shut down businesses, and throw people out of work. It also reconfigured how many of us live, recalibrating expectations and requiring new habits. Probably the most impactful lifestyle change was how COVID-19 ushered in—or at the least galvanized—a new era in the employment sector where workers, when given (or demanding) the option, opted for full-time or part-time (hybrid) remote working situations. Bringing a paradigm shift in the labor market, the pandemic drove the development of a stay-at-home work subculture.[233]

In a recent article, *Forbes* stated that almost 98 percent of workers want to work remote some of the time, 65 percent all the time, 32 percent part of the time, 57 percent of workers are inclined to seek new employment if their current gig doesn't allow them the remote option, and that by 2025, 32.6 million Americans—about 22 percent of the workforce—will report to work from a coveted remote location.[234]

There are other statistics out there that can be spun, but it is undeniable that, as Bob Dylan sang, the times, they are a-changin'.

While the onset of commonplace remote work has brought many changes to the economy—e.g., relocation of workers, changes in real estate prices, downscaling of businesses in central cities and downtowns, and new opportunities to work—for present purposes, the major impact has been, and by all indications will continue to be, on public transportation. Bloomberg described the new order in stark and succinct terms: "The post-pandemic reality for America's public transportation is bleak. Work from home has solidly set in, leaving transit agencies that rely on fare-box revenue facing a fiscal cliff."[235]

In consequence, local governments across the land have thrust their hands out begging for financial help. The thinking is that without bailout monies, ticket prices will increase and inevitable drastic cuts to service frequencies will upset commuter schedules and, in some sectors, expansions will get jettisoned. It has become a national movement of "please show me the money." For example, New York's Metropolitan Transportation Authority implored its political servants in Albany for a massive bailout—and lo and behold, it got one.[236]

The Bay Area is center stage with the problem.

Bob Spotswood, a political writer for the *Marin Independent Journal*, former mayor of the town of Mill Valley and former Director of the Golden Gate Bridge, Highway & Transportation District, echoed what many in the nation have concluded: "The pandemic changed everything for Bay Area transit agencies. Remote working once seemed utopian. Now, it's the new normal for office workers and professionals."[237]

Not surprisingly, therefore, with dark clouds on the horizon, the California Transit Association asked its political contingent in Sacramento for (and Governor Gavin Newson agreed to) a $5.15 billion bailout, spread over five years, for operating and construction subsidies to avoid threatened cuts in transit operations. In addition, according to the Metropolitan Transportation Commission (MTC), the interconnected transit agencies in the Bay Area have in mind asking voters once again to absorb the fiscal impact of remote work on the transit systems. Apparently, the strategy is to place on the California ballot, no sooner than 2026, a measure that will impose yet another tax increase to cover all or a portion of their financial shortfall.[238]

Some argue that the current crisis in public transportation is the result of the pandemic and this too shall pass.[239] That, it seems, is head-in-the-sand thinking. The decline of transit ridership in the United States was not an anomaly of the pandemic. It was underway and gaining speed before COVID-19 descended upon us.

For example: “The [BART] system had some of the nation’s lowest usage rates for major metropolitan areas before anyone ever heard of Covid-19. Transit systems had lost around 20 percent of their riders between 2014 and 2018. The only major transit system showing growth before the pandemic was Seattle’s. California’s systems’ ridership numbers have fallen more than most.”

One researcher captured it this way: “The pandemic has dramatically accelerated a broader decline in public transit use across the nation . . . [coming] after five years of falling transit patronage nationwide”[240]

Regardless of what studies are favored, what transit systems are showcased, or what political values are implicated in problem-solving channels, blaming COVIID-19 for the current systemic woes is clutching at straws. It is not as if agencies have suffered an interim hiccup that will come and go and once gone will enjoy restored health.

Public transit agencies can, however, blame the pandemic for at least bad timing as well as incremental damage.

COVID set transit back further and, in many cases, exacerbated a near-terminal condition, driving many transit systems to, and, for some, over the edge. It inflicted a more crushing blow to transit ridership than any other intervening occurrence the past hundred years, including the events of 9/11, driving transit overall ridership to a hundred-year low in 2020.[241] Of course, the effect on different local transit systems has varied, e.g., with greater longer-term injury to systems serving high-income riders (like in Marin and Sonoma counties) than those serving low-income riders.[242]

SMART has been fortunate in one respect. Its ridership numbers in response to the pandemic, on the whole, have rebounded better than some, aided in part by its buying of riders described in the preceding chapter. Initially, as it acknowledged, the pandemic had "devastating" effect "from a ridership and fare collection perspective."[243] But it gradually recovered a significant portion of lost ridership. For example, after finding itself deeper in the hole thanks to the pandemic, SMART in fiscal year 2022 saw ridership nearly triple the prior fiscal year.[244] And between fiscal year 2023 and 2024, SMART enjoyed an increase in ridership of 36 percent.[245]

But taking nothing away from the efforts that aided recovery, SMART, like the rest of the transit systems in the nation, continues to face the added limitations the pandemic and remote work movement have injected into transit systems.

While the numbers vary depending on the study, the general consensus seems to be that while ridership generally is back to about 80 percent of what it was before the pandemic, it appears that a return to the old days is not in the cards. Former Transportation Secretary Pete Buttigieg observed: "Even three years since the shutdowns began, we have not yet landed at our new normal. We're not going back to 2019."[246]

The New York Times explored the topic of continued remote impact, asking several experts to opine on the prospects whether remote work will remain at current levels or change. The consensus that emerged from the research posited that present levels were likely to stay as they are, in the range of 25 percent.[247]

The US Survey of Working Arrangements and Attitudes found that workers who could perform their job duties from home preferred doing just that about three days a week, preferring to avoid the time and costs of commuting, among other benefits of the remote workplace. In response, employers pretty much caved, allowing them to stay home about 2–3 days a week.[248]

The Bay Area is no different.

The Bay Area Council, a local business association that coordinates regional economic development, conducted a survey of over a hundred employers in early 2023 to gain insight into return-to-work (RTO) trends in the Bay Area. Among other things, it learned that by March 2023:

- About 70 percent of the surveyed workforce would return to the office three days a week with 28 percent not at all.
- Eighty-one percent of the surveyed workforce would not come to work on Thursdays and Fridays.
- Twenty-two percent of the surveyed workforce would be "fully remote."[249]

The changes in the employment sector have taken different forms. Chief among them is offering employees a hybrid model of work attendance, with some days in the office, some not. In 2023, for example, about one-third of job openings in San Francisco included a hybrid or fully remote work option compared with 5 percent in 2019, which puts San Francisco at the top of the fifty largest cities in the nation.[250]

Interestingly, since the onset of COVID and the increase of remote work, commuters have increasingly opted to drive rather than use public transit. According to one study, in 2022, almost 80 percent of vehicle trips were with one passenger or via a ride-hail vehicle, an increase of almost 14 percent from 2019. Audrey Denis of Cubic Transportation

Systems observed: "People are still opting to drive if they do have to execute a commute."[251]

One CEO put it more bluntly: "There's this assumption that people like commuting into a central business district," Mark Dixon, CEO of flexible office company IWG said. "They don't. It's a complete waste of time and money and they don't want to do it."[252]

In fact, the recent uptick in ridership coming out of the worst of the pandemic is evidently occurring in the middle of the week when traffic congestion is less, suggesting that the recovery will have little or no impact on the related traffic congestion problems that plague the nation, including in the North Bay. Robert Puentes, president of Eno Center for Transportation in Washington, D.C., noted: "We've seen that the normal workweek has changed fundamentally."[253] To the extent that trend continues and bleeds into Marin and Sonoma counties, SMART will suffer all the more in pursuit of its mission as it gets further distanced than it already is from its Pollyannaish goal to relieve traffic congestion.

The trend is away from public transit and toward getting in cars.

The public transit mentality is survival, regardless of the bona fides of the system and cost-benefit factors. Much of the dialogue for how to save public transit focuses on changing the nature of the service, catering to riders not in their sweet spot. As one article put it:

> The riders transit agencies have catered to for decades are also the ones who abandoned their systems in droves, and some transportation officials are facing a difficult prospect: To win back straphangers, they must remake public transit to better serve everyone whose lives don't revolve around traveling into a central business district.

> But the very issue pressuring them to do so—a dramatic decline in ridership that's left the largest systems with less than 70 percent of their pre-pandemic traffic even now—is also the biggest obstacle to innovation. Public transit is facing a financial rut that's spurred their CEOs to press city and state governments for new funding streams and taxes.[254]

That resonates with what SMART is trying to do as discussed in the prior chapter, moving closer toward to a heavily subsidized recreational system, inflating a class of riders that were not the core focus of the system when the legislature created the SMART district and when SMART appealed to local taxpayers to finance the system.

For how long and in what forms will these recent negative repercussions endure?

While it is fair to say the jury is still out on how long the COVID-induced remote working changes will last and with it the long-term impact on public transit, current indications suggest that the new world order is here to stay. The remote story—finding the balance between remote and RTO—still has content yet written, as many questions remain. For example, where in the mix of remote, hybrid, and RTO will a sustained balance be found? How will it get determined? To what extent will it get resolved through classic labor and management interplay? To what extent will it change or redistribute residential concentrations? Have we seen the worst of the pandemic's scaling back of public transit? What will be the long-term impact of remote work on traffic congestion in the North Bay?

But posing these questions should not blind civic leaders to the writing on the wall glaring at them. Many in the public sector wax enthusiastic, even evangelistic, about public transit. At a threshold level, that is understandable. There is much to commend its role in our culture. The problem often is, however, that those in positions of power and influence often have tunnel vision in assessing the merits and utility of transit systems, especially those in which their public egos are invested, and bring an almost unchecked compulsion to dedicating public monies to projects they have long trumpeted.

But in the same way that medications can mask mental and physical conditions, massive government subsidies can mask the terminally ill transit system. Public transit is in serious decline. Some transit systems are on life support. SMART is a prime example.

Do taxpayers want to spend billions of dollars on a poorly performing transit system or would they prefer to spend limited funds on other pressing needs?

10

The Burn-the-Boats Strategy

Historical annals recount that in the sixteenth century, the infamous conquistador and renowned military strategist Hernán Cortés, after landing in Veracruz, Mexico, ordered his men to burn the ships that transported them to prevent any possible retreat to Cuba, in furtherance of his campaign to conquer the Aztec Empire. The strategy birthed the idiom *burning the boats*, a do-or-die gambit.

In modern terms, this phenomenon is known as *escalating commitment*—a high-stakes decision that shuts off alternative paths. Closely related to the sunken cost fallacy (see chapter 13), escalating commitment captures the misjudgment leaders make when they continue pouring resources into a failing course of action, even in the face of unmistakable evidence that the project is no longer viable, effective, or worth the cost, to justify previous actions or avoid admitting error and foreclose a reversal.

Consider the California High-Speed Rail project, originally sold to voters as a sleek link between San Francisco and Los Angeles, to be completed by 2020 for $33 billion. Today, the cost has ballooned to more than $100 billion—and continues to rise. The project remains in limbo, with only a portion of the Central Valley segment (Merced to Bakersfield) partially under construction and mired in delays. Billions have already been spent on land acquisition, environmental reviews, legal battles, and incomplete infrastructure.

California had more modest, cost-effective alternatives—such as upgrading Amtrak service or investing in bus rapid transit—but rejected them. Now, with billions already committed, the state is doubling down, funneling resources into the Central Valley segment under the pretense of a "proof of concept."

The reality is starker: the state has no politically or financially viable exit.

Backing out would mean returning at least $3.5 billion in early federal grants, and potentially another $4 billion from more recent funding—an option deemed politically suicidal. Further complicating any retreat is the creation of an entire bureaucratic apparatus (the California High-Speed Rail Authority), a slew of ballot measures, legislative acts, and multilateral agreements that have entrenched the project despite plummeting public confidence. California's high-speed rail has devolved to less about transportation and more about salvaging political face.

So, California burned the boats and forged doggedly ahead.

Faced with their own legacy of failure, SMART encountered their burn-the-boats crossroads in choosing whether to push ahead with costly commuter rail extensions to Windsor, Healdsburg, and Cloverdale despite a dismal track record that portended more of the same.

SMART launched the northern expansion with service to Windsor clinging to a farebox recovery ratio that hovered around 6 percent, which underscored its overwhelming reliance on subsidies—especially sales taxes—rather than rider-generated revenue. In practical terms, the system was nowhere near self-sustaining. From a business standpoint, SMART was financially insolvent, fundamentally nonviable, and effectively unbankable—on a trajectory toward collapse. Worse, no meaningful turnaround was in sight. If anything, its operating position was poised to deteriorate further.

In practical terms, six cents of every dollar that SMART spends on operations comes from rider fares; the remaining 94 percent comes from taxpayers. The situation is even worse than those numbers reveal. Year after year, SMART has slashed fares—today they are nearly 50 percent lower than in 2018—and has offered free rides to select groups in a transparent attempt to inflate ridership and fabricate an illusion of success. Even with these artificial boosts, SMART has never reached the ridership levels promised when they sought public funding. It has consistently failed to meet projections for both total fare revenue and farebox recovery ratio. Yet remarkably, SMART continues to project future revenues that surpass every previous year except 2020—a claim that defies both history and credibility. The public can rest assured the costs of the extensions will continue to rise.

No data has suggested a surge of riders in the north. Prior expansions didn't deliver promised surges in fare revenue. Extending service north to Windsor, Healdsburg, and eventually Cloverdale means more trains in service, more staff, more maintenance, and more subsidy dependency without a clear path to greater revenue. The northerly regions have lower population densities, with no major growth potential, and weaker transit demand. That translates to fewer riders, longer distances, and higher per-rider costs—and lower farebox recovery ratios. The consistently near-empty parking lot near the Windsor station speaks volumes.

The cost of the north expansion is disproportionate to the paltry ridership numbers. The Windsor extension projects a $70 million expenditure and so far has spent $35 million. The Healdsburg piece projects a $160 million expenditure and SMART so far has shelled out $78 million. The cost of extending service to Cloverdale is projected at $308 million.

Moreover, SMART has openly admitted (see chapter 13) that without reaching deeper into the wallets of local taxpayers through a sales tax extension, it faces imminent collapse—running out of operating funds unless rescued by a massive bailout.

The agency finds itself in a political corner of its own making. They lured the public into subsidizing a sprawling rail project stretching from San Rafael to Cloverdale, binding itself to a promise it cannot break without shattering trust. By that point, SMART had already sunk millions into environmental reviews, right-of-way upgrades, and station planning for Windsor and Healdsburg—securing state and federal grants specifically earmarked for northern service. Abandoning the northern expansion would have betrayed that commitment and doomed any chance of future sales tax renewals and grant funding. In effect, SMART eliminated the possibility of scaling back.

So SMART "burned the boats," hoping to foreclose retreat.

Here is the other side of the problem.

When taxpayers in communities like Marin and Sonoma counties keep funding a failing project, they are diverting funds from critical needs like housing, education, the environment, health care, infrastructure, and public safety. Sidestepping opportunities in those areas has a long-term compound effect on community well-being. Further, pouring money down a bottomless pit like SMART can easily lead to budget deficits, cuts in essential services, or increased reliance on debt.

Marin and Sonoma residents are engaged in their communities. They tend to scrutinize public spending. When their elected leaders throw good money after bad, they lose confidence in leadership, which in this political climate is a rapidly evaporating asset and can depress civic engagement and support for future initiatives. Officials who double down rather than recalibrate undermine public pride and perpetuate a governance culture that elevates ego and face-saving over intelligent and courageous course corrections.

The expansion of SMART to Windsor, Healdsburg, and Cloverdale is a wasteful and foolhardy use of public monies. Despite the repeated promises of ameliorating traffic congestion and promoting effective, efficient, and widely used sustainable transit, the SMART system has underperformed grossly in ridership and farebox recovery. Extending the line northward into sparely populated community pockets with limited transit demand only exacerbates that imbalance, diverting millions of taxpayer dollars from higher-priority needs.

The expansion is a textbook case of escalating commitment—a refusal to reassess in the face of mounting evidence that the project is financially unjustifiable, unsustainable, and misaligned with the region's shifting transportation needs and demographics. Instead, leaders persist in spending scarce tax dollars in a futile attempt to "prove it will work," clinging to a fantasy rather than reality. Admitting failure would have been a rare but commendable act of accountability. Instead, under no legal compulsion to expand, in a time of fiscal constraint, SMART chose to double down on a marginal service, a choice as imprudent as it is reckless.

11

Rigging the Rules

Politicians are, if nothing else, buoyant. They are nature's finest chameleons, changing colors not to blend into their surroundings, but to stand out just enough to secure votes, dodge accountability, and, of course, keep those donations flowing. One moment they are championing fiscal restraint; the next they're greenlighting billion-dollar pork projects like it is a clearance sale. One moment, they are robust in the fight for voters' rights; the next they are spouting about election integrity and democracy while they rewrite thresholds and access rules to prevent votes from spoiling the plot twist. Their resilience is unmatched—and in fairness, quite impressive—truth, after all, is flexible when the next election peers around the corner. Principles? They are more like menu specials: available for a limited time, subject to polling data and the latest political agenda.

As outlined in chapter 1, SMART proponents suffered a long legislative campaign to convince the public to fund their ambitious commuter rail project with hard-earned taxpayer dollars. The effort reached a turning point in 2020, when voters decisively rejected Measure I—the first attempt to extend the sales tax originally approved under Measure Q in 2008 for another thirty years. This time, voters weren't buying into projections or promises or sleight of hand. They had a record to evaluate. They could judge SMART's operational and administrative performance—and they did. The verdict was clear: no more blank checks.

But rather than accept that outcome, rather than honor the will of the electorate, the politicians hatched a simple plan: change the rules.

Out of the darkness in Sacramento slithered SB 904, a piece of legislation that State Senator Bill Dodd authored exclusively for SMART, which became law in September 2024, codified in Section 20355.1 of the Public Contract Code. SB 904 authorizes voter-initiated ballot measures in Marin and Sonoma Counties to propose extensions of the 2008 Measure Q sales tax—removing the prior restriction that only the SMART board could place such measures on the ballot. More significantly, it allows any proposed tax extension to pass by a simple majority, bypassing the traditional two-thirds requirement for special taxes. In effect, SB 904 substantially lowers the bar for approval and opens the door for SMART to sidestep the will of the voters—who have repeatedly rejected or narrowly approved such taxes, making it easier to lock in decades of continued funding.

When politicians rewrite the rules to achieve a political outcome unattainable under an existing process, they cross a fundamental line in democratic governance. Such is the case when legislators lower the voter approval threshold for a specific tax measure after voters have repeatedly rejected predecessor measures. That maneuver, often disguised, as here, as a courageous step to reclaim democracy, is in truth a calculated circumvention of voter will.

The two-thirds vote requirement was established to ensure bipartisan consensus on tax increases, to serve as a check against the influence of well-funded special interests in local elections, and to compel local governments to demonstrate a clear and compelling need for any proposed public project funded with special sales taxes. Voters have repeatedly affirmed their support for this higher threshold when it comes to special taxes. And when voters decline to approve a tax multiple times under these rules, their message is clear: there's insufficient support. To respond by lowering the bar mocks voters, sending the message that their vote only counts when aligned with the preferences of those in power—a message that Washington sends each day in painful increments.

It also constitutes an admission. Rather than persuading more taxpayers of the merits of a sale tax extension measure, elected officials instead tilted the system to produce the result they want. That is not leadership; it is manipulation.

It's true that democracy is grounded in majority rule—but that's only part of the equation. Democracy isn't just about who wins. It's also about *how* decisions are made. It relies on clear, consistent rules, the protection of minority rights, and the processes that ensure legitimacy. When a supermajority threshold has a long history, especially for decisions that impose long-term financial burdens on local taxpayers, it's because those decisions require broader consensus. That *too* is a democratic value. And rule-changing to undermine repeated prior results is *anti* democratic.

Recall (see chapter 1) that voters rejected the sales tax measure *five* times. The first attempt, in 1990, saw officials try to game the system by labeling it a "general tax," which only needed majority approval. It failed anyway. In 1998, the measure lost again, earning less than 50 percent of the vote. In 2000, Sonoma County bypassed Marin County entirely and went it alone—but nearly 60,000 voters rejected the plan and it failed. In 2006, the proposal failed yet again, with 95,000 votes against. In 2008, proponents devised a new strategy: instead of requiring two-thirds approval in each of the two counties, they decided to combine vote totals. Knowing Marin taxpayers were skeptical, they relied on heavier support in Sonoma, the main beneficiaries of the commuter rail line, to push it through. The measure passed, even though Marin voters—who would shoulder much of the tax burden while reaping fewer benefits—rejected it with less than two-thirds support. Finally, in 2020, Measure I, which sought to extend the tax for three decades, met a resounding defeat, with **more than 135,000** negative votes.

The SB 94 gambit draws from the gerrymander playbook. At its core, gerrymandering is about manipulating electoral boundaries to tilt the outcome in favor of one party or interest group—undermining the principle of fair representation. California's SB 904, though focused on taxation rather than district lines, operates with a strikingly similar intent and effect. Both are tools used by those in power to sidestep the well-expressed will of voters when the democratic process doesn't yield the desired result.

Consider this comment by a justice of the Ohio Supreme Court in striking down a Republican gerrymander scheme to redraw district lines for partisan gain: "When the dealer stacks the deck in advance, the house usually wins." That warning echoes loudly here.

Changing the rules after repeated defeats at the ballot box risks disenfranchising the tens of thousands of voters in both Marin and Sonoma counties who have said "no" to extending the sales tax that funds SMART. In 2020, more than **135,000** taxpayers rejected Measure I—an emphatic message that the public was no longer willing to subsidize the commuter rail system for another three decades. Overriding that verdict by lowering the voting threshold silences the voices of those who participated in the voting process in good faith, believing that their votes would count. True democracy means respecting the outcome—even when it's inconvenient for those in power.

12

The Unfairness of It All

In every generation, a clamor for justice is heard when taxes fall hardest on those least able to pay. The 1773 Boston Tea Party, often seen as a protest against taxation without representation, was fundamentally opposition to an economic system that favored the wealthy at the expense of regular colonists. The British government had forced locals to subsidize a bailout of the East India Company, the genesis of the regressive tax system.

Those dynamics have played out for centuries.

In 1999, voters in Washington State passed Initiative 695 that repealed a vehicle excise tax. Though the court ultimately struck the measure—not on its merits but by invoking constitutional procedural grounds—its popularity reflected a public revolt against flat, usage-based taxes that disproportionately hit working families—especially in rural and suburban areas.

More recently, a soda tax in Philadelphia, a well-intentioned measure designed to fund pre-K programs, ran into a fierce backlash from low-income communities, who pointed out that lower-income households had to disproportionately bear the charge for a social good—early education—that should be publicly funded through fair, progressive means. The measure remains controversial and divisive.

Regressive taxes repeatedly ignite resistance because they offend the social contract. They punish people of lesser means by shifting responsibility for those taxes from those with greater financial resources to those with the least. One key lesson from history is that taxation should be rooted in justice—a principle that the modern Congress and Executive Branch have abandoned like a broken oath.

In practical terms, the *effective* tax rate of a regressive tax decreases as income increases, meaning lower-income taxpayers shell out a *larger percentage* of their income in taxes compared to higher-income taxpayers. That is because regressive taxes—such as sales taxes, excise taxes, and flat fees—typically are applied uniformly without any adjustment for the taxpayer's ability to pay. Simply put, while everyone might pay the same amount, with the sales tax embedded in the purchase price for goods, the sales price takes a bigger chunk of a lower-income person's paycheck than it does for someone with greater earnings. So, the less money the taxpayer makes, the more unfair the tax feels.

The sales tax that finances SMART's administration and operations, in addition to interest on bonds issued years before—the same sales tax SMART will soon implore voters to extend for thirty years—is an archetypal regressive tax because it disproportionately and unfairly impacts lower-income residents in Marin and Sonoma Counties. By its nature, the sale tax applies uniformly to all consumers in the two counties regardless of income levels, which means, by definition, that lower-income residents will pay a greater percentage of their income toward the tax than wealthier residents.

That burden is especially unjust considering that lower-income residents are among the least likely to benefit directly from the commuter rail system. Many cannot afford to live nor work near the limited and primarily suburban stations, nor can they easily adjust their work schedules around its infrequent service. For example, according to federal Census bureau data, youth and seniors collectively represent 42 percent of the population of Sonoma and Marin Counties, yet they account for only about 12 percent of SMART's ridership, virtually all of them now riding for free, approximately 110,000 riders in FY 2025.[255] White-collar professionals dominate weekday peak-hour trips and leisure riders the off-peak hour weekend. In effect, the tax forces the working poor and many fixed-income seniors who don't ride the train to help subsidize a commuter rail system that primarily serves wealthier residents who live and work along the corridor, and also more likely to have cars and flexible schedules, shifting the cost of a public amenity onto those least able to afford it.

Flat sales taxes are often sold to the public as fair and efficient: a uniform rate applied to the purchase of goods that generates revenue without the complications of income-based taxation. But that sales pitch is disingenuous. Beneath the veneer of neutrality, a flat sales tax becomes fundamentally inequitable when applied to fund services that a narrow slice of a population will enjoy. This is especially unfair for communities like Marin and Sonoma, where everyone pays for a service so little used. The result is a gross distortion of fiscal fairness and a misalignment of public responsibility.

What's more, because income inequality is often correlated with race and geography, regressive sales taxes reinforce systemic disparities. Communities of color with higher poverty rates end up contributing disproportionately to public revenues through consumption taxes, yet they receive less investment in return—through poorer infrastructure, schools, and health-care access. The structure of a regressive tax amplifies existing inequalities.

This problem is widespread. States have raised sales taxes to fund sports arenas, convention centers, niche cultural venues, or specialty transit systems that a small segment of the population use. In many cases, these services are located far from lower-income neighborhoods, require fees to access, or are simply irrelevant to the lives of many taxpayers. The sales tax is easily collected and politically expedient, but its true cost is masked in everyday transactions.

There are countless ways to illustrate the disparities. The hypotheticals that follow draw on assumptions consistent with the demographics of Marin and Sonoma Counites. Changing those assumptions, e.g., increasing or decreasing average annual income or estimated spending levels, will not change the result. In all cases, the data will show a pattern: the less money an individual or family makes, the higher percentage of their income they pay to fund SMART.

Each of the following hypothetical residents of Marin and Sonoma Counties pays a quarter-cent sales tax to fund SMART operations. The income and spending numbers are conservative for illustration.

Luis earns $35,000 annually and spends $22,000 for taxable goods. Luis will pay $55 in SMART sales taxes each year or **.16 percent** of his income.

Della earns $55,000 annually and spends $30,000 on taxable goods. Della will pay more in SMART sales taxes than Luis ($75) each year but a lower percentage of her income (**.14 percent**).

Joan earns $90,000 annually and spends $38,000 for taxable goods. Joan will pay more in SMART sales taxes than

Luis and Della ($95) each year but a lower percentage of her income (**.11 percent**) than either of them.

Jerry earns $160,000 annually and spends $45,000 for taxable goods. Jerry will pay more in SMART sales taxes ($112.50) than Luis, Della, and Joan each year and a lower percentage (**.07 percent**) of his income.

Finally, Sheldon earns $300,000 annually and spends $50,000 for taxable goods. Sheldon will pay more in SMART sales taxes than all the others ($125) each year, but a lower percentage (**.04 percent**) than all of them.

Here is a corresponding table.[256]

Income Group	**Average Annual Income**	**Estimated Spending on Taxable Goods**	**¼ cent Sales Tax Paid**	**% of Income Paid on SMART Sales Tax**
Low-Income	$35,000	$22,000	$55	.16%
Working Class	$55,000	$30,000	$75	.14%
Middle Class	$90,000	$38,000	$95	.11%
Upper Middle	$160,000	$45,000	$112.50	.07%
High-Income	$300,000	$50,000	$125	.04%

In the prior "Expenditure Plan" SMART circulated to support the failed the Measure I ballot, SMART projected that $2 billion would be collected over the life of the extension. According to projections from the California Department of Finance, that meant the average household in each of Marin and Sonoma Counties would spend thousands of dollars over thirty years to subsidize passengers to take SMART trains. Based on rough estimates, the thirty-year sales tax extension

SMART wants taxpayers to approve over the life of the extension will likely cost Marin households almost $9,000 and Sonoma households almost $7,000 and on a per capita basis about $4,000 in Marin and about $3,000 in Sonoma.

The inequity is inescapable.

Finally, sales taxes, including those that fund SMART, are often invisible to the average consumer at the point of sale of goods. While marketed as a modest, voter-approved measure to support public transportation, and with the promise that "businesses will pay a substantial share of the tax," the structure of the tax conceals its genuine cost and unfair impact. Unlike income or property taxes—where taxpayers receive a bill or fill out a form—sales taxes are seamlessly embedded into the purchase price of goods, even nontaxable goods and services. It's a mechanism of deception. When consumers in Marin and Sonoma buy school supplies, bottled water, children's clothes, work uniforms, toilet paper, cosmetics, cell phones and accessories, toys, books, fuel (on top of the excise tax), a sandwich, a pair of running or hiking shoes, or any item of clothing, among many other consumer items, the tax is not itemized. It's silently absorbed into the purchase price. When politicians have urged voters to fund SMART with a sales tax, voters saw meaningless numbers flash by, a half cent here, a quarter cent there. But in time, over the course of decades, the fractions add up to real money as shown, a river of pennies feeding a massive reservoir of dollars. Taxpayers never feel their weight, much like they don't feel the disproportionate nature of the regressive sales tax.

Because the taxes are hidden, voters cannot make informed decisions about the individual costs of a tax extension in real dollars and a percentage of net income. The lack of transparency undermines democratic oversight and allows public projects like SMART to escape rigorous cost-benefit evaluation where it matters the most: the impact on the voter.

On the surface, the SMART sales tax may seem minor to some, but its regressive structure and hidden nature reduce the tax to an ignoble and divisive policy tool. Taxation should be transparent, based on vertical and horizontal equity, and grounded in democratic legitimacy.

Public figures across the political spectrum—like President Franklin Delano Roosevelt, US Senators Bernie Sanders, Paul Wellston, and Elizabeth Warren, US Representative Ron Paul, Commentator Pat Buchanan, the Reverend Martin Luther King Jr., Fox News Commentator Sean Hannity, and former Secretary of Labor Robert Reich—have decried the regressive tax as a form of injustice.

Nobel Prize–winning economist Joseph Stiglitz put it this way: "A tax system that relies heavily on consumption taxes shifts the burden from the rich to the poor. It's a backdoor way to gut redistribution."

13

The Future of SMART

Might the SMART train project be barreling toward a fatal political collision? If so, it should not come as a shock or even a surprise to anyone tracking the historical performance of the suburban rail system. Except for a decline in ridership courtesy of the Pandemic, virtually out of the gate and continuing, SMART performance flattened at a water-treading level, kept afloat in the main by increases in local tax revenue, raising the specter of a ruinous reckoning.

The authors of the legislation that spawned the SMART District and launched the rail system exhibited some caution by covering bases should SMART display a finite shelf life. The enabling legislation included a separate chapter titled "Dissolution" that laid out a procedure for unwinding the SMART District if things did not pan out.[257]

The legislation provides two separate ways to call it a day, each appropriately putting the fate of the SMART District in the hands of voters. The SMART board may call for an election to allow voters to decide whether to dissolve and unwind the District or voters may do the same via a petition that places the same measure on the ballot, qualifying with a minimum of twenty-five (25) percent of the total vote cast at the last general statewide election.[258]

In either case, the ballot measure puts to voters a pithy yes-or-no question: "Shall the Sonoma-Marin Area Rail Transit District be dissolved?"

Approval requires a simple majority.[259] If the measure passes, the SMART board must adopt a resolution dissolving the SMART District and proceed to unwind its business.[260] The statute also directs how SMART property should be divvied up.[261]

These statutory provisions, once perhaps precautionary, became a genuine thing when the Marin County Civil Grand Jury in a 2023 report issued a call to arms that jolted SMART into getting real about where things stand. The grand jury titled its report, "SMART at a Crossroads, Here Today, Gone Tomorrow." It kicked off its dissection of the situation with a wake-up call: "What is [SMART's] plan to continue operations after April 2029 when essential revenue from the ¼ percent sales tax expires?"

The Marin County Grand Jury highlighted its concerns with several bottom-line comments, namely that:

- Local taxpayers have poured "over $600,000 million" into the SMART operation (a subset of over $1 billion spent overall).
- Ridership "remains short of expectations."
- SMART "has never" met its goal of funding thirty-six (36) percent of annual operating costs with commuter fares.
- Without a spike in ridership, "the public may not be convinced of SMART's value."

- And, most ominously, SMART "is highly dependent on sales tax revenues for its operations" and "will likely be forced to discontinue services if Marin and Sonoma county voters do not approve a sales tax extension by the required supermajority in an election before 2029."[262]

The grand jury also zeroed in on the Achilles' heel that has and will forever plague the SMART commuter rail program:

> SMART is a system that, in contrast to other Bay Area transit agencies, has fewer potential riders, operates on a route with stops that are not close to many residences or large employment centers, and its route is such that it does not serve as many commuters as do other public transit agencies.[263]

As discussed, that systemic flaw—a lack of concentration of employment centers and widely diffused residential communities typical of suburbia that guaranteed a perpetually low ceiling on ridership—is why SMART flattened quickly and became doomed from the beginning. SMART in consequence will never function in a cost-effective manner. It will always require massive infusion of funds to function grossly disproportionate to its ridership numbers and meager benefits. If SMART were a for-profit business, a bankruptcy petition would have followed as a matter of course.

When the grand jury flashed the writing on the wall, SMART retreated into self-introspection and, for the first time, injected the "D" word—dissolution—into its planning and discourse. In response to the Marin County Civil Grand Jury concerns, under the guidance of its CFO, Heather

McKillop, SMART devised three short-term outcomes: a "base plan" and two alternative scenarios.[264]

The Base Plan

This plan embraces the status quo, painting a rosy picture of the future. It incorporates the capital plan the SMART board approved several years ago, with customary updates as SMART receives grant dollars and as sales tax estimates change and assumes existing service levels. The base plan, however, is grounded in a vital assumption, the hope that voters will extend the existing sales tax they approved in 2008 (but rejected in 2020), gifting SMART $51.5 million annually in voter generated revenue beginning in fiscal year 2030. In presenting the base plan to the board, the SMART CFO noted that the "sales tax is the number one funding source for transit agencies around the country."[265]

Alternative Scenario # 1

This scenario assumes that voters do *not* extend local sales taxes prior to fiscal year 2029, that service levels stay roughly the same as the base plan into fiscal year 2030, and that SMART runs out of money to operate by fiscal year 2030, leaving only legally untouchable funds to satisfy employment benefit and pension obligations. SMART acknowledges it would be highly unlikely to gain access to "an extra $60 million" to replace the lost sales tax revenue and that, as a result, it would have to split up its assets and resolve its governmental commitments.[266]

The SMART CFO dubbed this unhappy path "the full steam ahead" scenario,[267] meaning, effectively, that facing its demise, SMART would go down in a blaze of spendthrift glory, spending all its money. As she unabashedly put it: it is "where we just run [the program] into the ground."[268] In other words, knowing the end is near, SMART would exhaust all financial resources, if only because, well, it could, rather than stockpiling funds for other community purposes the legislature might identify and authorize.

Alternative Scenario # 2

This alternative also assumes that taxpayers do not extend the local sales tax prior to fiscal year 2029. In scenario #2, however, SMART drastically reduces service levels after fiscal year 2028 by at least half, similar to the levels that existed during the pandemic. The difference between Scenario #2 and the pandemic is that SMART in Scenario #2 would drastically reduce staff, which ran full during the pandemic, and suffer an approximately 50 percent reduction in ridership with the attendant reduction in fare revenue.

Retention of staff in those unstable circumstances, however, is more complex and less formulaic than SMART may think. While it is hard to know precisely how the next few years will play out, an increasingly shaky future puts SMART staff in an untenable situation. As time goes on, and the drumbeat of a shaky SMART future gets louder, employees will be faced with whether to remain on a potentially sinking ship. As any failing business knows, when choppy seas threaten survival, individuals tend to bail, no matter what assurances, cajoling, or pep talks they receive or efforts an employer uses to right the ship. Staff have lives to live, families to protect, and futures to rechart. As SMART takes on more and more water, employees may abandon ship in increasing numbers. And who could blame them?

The same slippery slope applies to non–sales tax funding sources. Public dollars are precious. Their deployment depends often on the highest and best use and well-considered and constantly recalibrated priorities. SMART appreciates this probability:

> Either people are going to stop giving . . . grants or we're not going to have the match to do it because we're going to need to save up that money to try to run services as long as possible. . . . and that happens in '27 where we basically say, "We can't go after any more grants, accept any more grants because we can't match them." . . . Even though we could continue to operate, it does not get us fulfilling what we originally told the voters as trying to get all of those projects done to include the pathways.[269]

The bottom line, as SMART acknowledges, is this:

> It's reasonable to assume that we need a sales tax extension and reauthorization prior to '29 . . . to carry out . . . our mission and vision. . . . Although it may be possible for another government entity to assume responsibility for SMART operations, it is not likely that passenger rail service could be operated for an extended period without a dedicated funding source. As a result, without a sales tax, staff assumes the District would be dissolved.[270]

Despite the thoughtfulness of SMART staff in constructing various forecasts, the entire analysis reduces to a simple proposition: no tax extension, no commuter rail system (in the absence of a conventional Sacramento-directed bailout). CFO McKillop told KTVU FOX 2 news that, without the taxpayer life raft, "We'll basically have to cease operation after 2029."[271]

Eddy Cumins, the SMART GM, agreed, advising the SMART board:

> SMART absolutely has to have a sales tax to continue operations. . . . You're talking about a doomsday scenario, I think there's also some thought that just another agency comes in and runs a passenger rail. I just want to be clear with the board, without a sales tax, that's not going to happen. There has to be a sales tax that's going to subsidize passenger rail in this area.[272]

Cumins reiterated his doomsday pronouncement during an interview with *The Press Democrat* editorial board. They asked him: "How does SMART plan to continue operations without its sales tax?" He responded: "The answer is, we're not."[273]

How has SMART handled this so far?

In the wake of the Marin County Civil Grand Jury report, the SMART board announced support for a $301,800 marketing plan to ratchet up public relations and image. The initiative includes spending $175,000 on mailers, $50,000 on video production, and $76,800 on paid advertising. Curiously, SMART was quick to disclaim this spending as a ruse to muster taxpayer support for its failing enterprise, that no matter what others might think, it was not a disguised campaign for a tax renewal, critical to its survival.[274] Here's how Julia Gonzalez, the agency's marketing director, spun this latest spending initiative: "The desired outcome is that people will be versed in understanding what this agency means in terms of quality-of-life impact."[275]

Really?

What does the public not know about the professed SMART "quality-of-life impact"? SMART has flooded the local community for years with rhetoric, promotion, and claims about how SMART is the commuter rail game changer, through the use of voter ballot campaign literature, costly traffic, rail performance, and environmental studies, a series of "white papers," marketing initiatives, and media interviews, among other means. The raw truth is that this latest expenditure of public funds has nothing to do with educating the public and *everything* to do with currying tax extension support, an early, under the radar campaign to start the process of prying dollars out of local taxpayers. It is yet another instance where SMART wants the public to forget how the costs of its operation are prohibitive relative to the limited number of riders and how taxpayers, not commuters, primarily pay for the program. Instead, the public can expect a steady stream of starry-eyed promotions about how SMART will someday become what it has long aspired to be, an innovative commuter system that reaps earth-shattering environmental benefits, coaxes a flotilla of gas-guzzling cars off the road, and will become the coveted prototype for suburban commuter rail systems. And on and on.

***

Where does it all leave taxpayers? The prevailing view is that they hold the keys to the kingdom. But how much more can reasonably be asked of them? Has the taxpayer well run dry?

Don't underestimate the power of voter fatigue. For example, in a memo dated November 13, 2023, the Transportation Agency of Marin (TAM) disclosed a plan at the Metropolitan Transportation Commission (MTC) to devise a Regional Transportation Measure (RTM) to levy a tax to fund transportation capital projects and operating costs.[276] The concern, however, was it might not be "prudent" to include the measure on the November 2024 ballot for fear of competing with a Housing Bond measure that the Bay Area Housing Finance Authority (BAHFA) is likely to sponsor: "To avoid splitting votes or creating voter fatigue from supporting multiple tax measures, a two-year separation between the Housing Bond and the RTM is being considered by MTC as the advisable strategy."[277] To put it more cynically, the goal is to figure out how to lull local taxpayers into approving a tax measure down the road they would not likely approve in the current environment due to taxation overload.

Similarly, the *Argus-Courier* out of Petaluma recently identified challenges local politicians face with a ballot measure that seeks taxpayer funding for climate mitigation and adaptation projects. The paper noted that "voter approval of a climate tax is likely to be a very high bar," not because Sonoma residents do not champion climate change remediation, but because, among other things, they are drowning from taxation overload. A climate change tax would follow "a fire agency tax proposal next spring and go head-to-head with a childcare tax measure on the November 2024 ballot." In addition, "any new tax will be on top of several existing county sales taxes to preserve agriculture and open space, repair and maintain county roadways, fund mental health and homeless services, maintain and expand commuter rail service, and support county parks and libraries."[278]

Let's be clear. It is not as if the good folks of Marin and Sonoma have not done their fair share—and more—to support local tax measures.

The County of Marin boasts a history of taxation generosity.[279] For example, in recent times, Marin County voters approved:[280]

Year	Measure(s)	Sales Tax:
2011	D & F	General sales taxes
2012	A	To increase for open space
2013	C	For various public works and related services
2014	O	To improve local quality of life and essential services
2015	C	To enhance quality public safety and general services and infrastructure
2017	B	To obtain bonds to finance roadway improvements
2018	F	An extension for general revenue purposes (like flood/sea level rise/disaster preparedness, fire prevention, infrastructure improvements, 911 response, and senior/youth programs)
2022	R	To preserve essential services
2022	G	To maintain basic government services
2022	A	To maintain open space, parks, and sustainable agriculture
2022	L	For long-term financial viability and improve local quality of life and essential services
2022	J	To maintain and enhance general services and facilities

The people of Sonoma County have been equally generous. For example, in recent times, Sonoma voters approved:[281]

Year	Measure(s)	Sales Tax
2012	Y	Increase on the purchase of goods and services for five years
2018	M	Ten-year sales tax to support improvements for regional and neighborhood parks and natural areas
2022	DD, G, V, U, T, S, Q & O	Collection of sales taxes regarding public services (e.g., transportation, open space, emergency and essential services, domestic violence and public safety, natural disaster preparedness, mental health, addiction and homeless services, and transportation)
2024	H	Additional sales tax for fire prevention, emergency paramedic services, and disaster response

The winds of local altruism, however, are shifting. For example, voters recently rejected a measure to impose a sales tax to finance childcare for low-income families and the towns of Greenbrae and Kentfield turned away parcel taxes to improve medians and local schools, respectively. The *Marin Independent Journal* noted as well that local opposition has swelled against attempts to increase the limit for statewide sales taxes for transportation projects.[282]

The Bay Area News Group and Joint Venture Silicon Valley, an organization that includes the *Marin Independent Journal*, recently conducted a poll to test the public appetite for funding commuter rail systems. It found "little enthusiasm for the subsidies, and much less for the usual means—tax, toll and fare hikes," signaling a "new reluctance . . . to whip out the wallet and pay more for public transit."[283] And regarding tax measures crafted to improve quality of life, Dick Spotswood of the *Marin IJ* acutely observed: "voter patience is wearing thin."[284] Again, it is not because voters don't care. It is because they, like everyone else, have boundaries, a community perspective the *Marin IJ* captured this way: "Voting against these tax measures does not mean one doesn't care about children, the poor or the environment. It is about setting limits on spending and better prioritization."[285]

Case in point. A local resident and former member of the San Anselmo Planning Commission recently addressed the relentless procession of tax measures:

> I used to support almost every new tax. Taxes are good. I want government services and those cost money. I'll pay my fair share. I used to say all that. Now I say we need to rein in our local governments, agencies, and school districts to control new taxes and fees.[286]

Here is taxpayer-truth: Taxpayers have propped up a terminally ill SMART, which has spent more than $1 billion to create about three thousand weekday commuter trips, with fares covering about 6 percent of operating costs, with no reduction in traffic congestion and no demonstrated positive environmental impact. Worse, the sales tax voters approved in 2008 falls disproportionately on those who can least afford to shell out the money for the benefit of others to take recreational sojourns within the two counties. From a simple economic proposition, as a suburban commuter rail system, the costs of running the system compared with commuter usage levels and fares collected represent an obscene misuse of tax dollars that can never be justified, wholly part from the absence of any demonstrable reduction in traffic or greenhouse gas emissions.

SMART has been a colossal failure. SMART will always be a colossal failure. As difficult as it will be, given all the money spent, it is time to cut losses and stop asking taxpayers to fund this pipe dream.

SMART advocates will not go down without a fight, regardless of the merits. Be assured SMART advocates will seek to trigger anxiety about "sunk costs," proselytizing about how taxpayers are deep-in and beyond the point of no return. In other words, "don't dissolve us now, look at all the money you've invested."

In pure economic terms, sunk costs—funds spent that are not recoverable—are irrelevant to rational decision-making. Hence, the term "sunk." We all succumb to the fallacy of sunk costs in our personal lives, sticking with an activity that has outlived its usefulness and no longer makes sense. In the more routine sphere of our lives, it could be finishing a book that has profoundly disappointed us or finishing a restaurant meal we hated from the start, just because we have shelled out the money for them. It is not always easy to cut losses. So, we suffer the balance of the experience to avoid "wasting" the spent money.

Recall the infamous Concorde plane, a project launched in the mid-1950s and projected to reinvent air travel for an initial cost of $70 million. Over time, the airplane boondoggle cost more than $1 billion, as governments and private parties kept spending money hand over fist in the face of massive failings, repeatedly falling prey to the sunk cost fallacy. Eventually, the Concorde retired in 2003 and is now a novelty item, but not until hundreds of millions of dollars got poured into a proverbial rathole.

No one wants to appear wasteful and certainly politicians do not want to admit mistakes, especially one of the magnitude of SMART. The emotional reluctance is understandable. But rational decision-making should prevail. Voters can be the adults in the room.

Taxpayers in Marin and Sonoma who are disinclined to shell out more money to prop up SMART but do not want to see the commuter rail system scuttled probably need not worry. It is hard to imagine that if voters take a pass power brokers won't bail out rail service in the corridor in some manner. California is home to many politicians who are irreversibly committed to the proliferation of rail systems.

Perhaps the state will make riding on SMART free. That would be neither novel nor unprecedented. In fact, free public transit is starting to pick up steam nationwide. In 2023, Voice of America News published an article, "Free Public Transportation Accelerates in Some US Cities," noting that various cities have gone to zero-fare transit systems or are experimenting with narrowly defined zero-fare pilot programs, including Washington, D.C., Kansas City, Denver, Alexandria, Seattle, Portland, New York, and San Francisco.[287] The recent SMART decision to provide free transit to seniors and youth, while done to bolster ridership numbers for political reasons, is a possible step in this direction. As it is, Marin and Sonoma taxpayers subsidize 94 percent of SMART fares.

Perhaps more likely, the powers that be, who have a bounty of financial resources at their disposal, will simply pour more money into the project. Consider the cost overrun debacle and incessant delays associated with California high-speed rail. Those dyed-in-the-wool rail enthusiasts will likely not stand idle if taxpayers decline the invitation to throw good money after bad and could well lead the charge to rescue SMART, putting the financial onus on a wider berth of taxpayers, even statewide, or even businesses.

One possible source is California's Cap and Trade program. Simplified, under the program, the California Air Resources Board sets a ceiling on statewide green gashouse emissions each year and requires the prime emitters, e.g., oil refineries, electricity generators and importers, and manufacturing facilities, to comply with the program in a few ways, including purchasing permits or offsets to cover allowed emissions. For state programs, including transportation, the upshot is a revenue source to fund operations, which the legislature allocates each year.[288] Historically, more than half of cap-and-trade revenues have been invested in sustainable communities and clean transportation, including transit and intercity rail systems.[289]

Digging into other pockets to bail out SMART does not mean it is the right thing to do. From a cost-benefit perspective, the SMART commuter rail system will not improve. SMART will always be what SMART is. What you see is always what you will get. A state bailout would satisfy a political fix and serve a bureaucratic agenda, relegating SMART to prolonged life support. But at the least, if that becomes its fate, the residents of Marin and Sonoma Counties would no longer shoulder the financial brunt of the SMART boondoggle.

Conclusion

The End of the Line

The SMART commuter rail system was launched as a bold, eco-friendly vision for Northern California's future—a sleek, sustainable alternative to the congestion of Highway 101. But it was built on false hopes and misled voters about both the true cost of passenger rail and the limited ridership potential of a former freight rail line repurposed to serve largely suburban communities.

SMART has become a cautionary tale of a bloated underperforming transit system funded on the backs of the working class, delivering too little to too few for too great a cost.

Let's be honest: SMART has failed and no political spinning and bureaucratic cheerleading can alter that sobering reality.

At the heart of the failure is the regressive funding mechanism that uses sales taxes as a primary method of subsidizing operations, a method that burdens taxpayers with the least amount of resources to spare and least opportunity to gain the meager benefits SMART provides. Worse, the tax is concealed at the point of sale of goods, obscuring the depth of the financial load that taxpayers shoulder, especially those the train does not serve.

Ridership has consistently fallen short of projections, and even if those projections were somehow met, they would do nothing to address the issue voters care most about: worsening traffic congestion. Farebox recovery has been dismal. Despite enormous capital investment, the reach of the rail system remains astonishingly limited—and will remain so due to demographics and where people live. For the average consumer, SMART does not eliminate the car, it merely shortens a fraction of the drive, if even that.

SMART's touted environmental benefits ring hollow—after all, SMART runs on diesel, contributes to greenhouse gas emissions, and does nothing to reduce overall vehicle miles traveled in the region. The most stinging failure is that the rail system has not relieved congestion on Highway 101. The road remains clogged, while the train glides past largely empty.

And SMART's head-spinning cost—over $1 billion through FY 2024—is not just financial. The opportunity cost is huge. Each dollar funneled into SMART is a dollar lost to more flexible, equitable, and affordable transit options—like bus networks and subsidized ride-shares—not to mention more pressing needs for Marin and Sonoma Counties like affordable and workforce housing, wildfire prevention and climate resilience, mental health and homeless services, infrastructure repair, schools and early child development, drought management and sea-level rise adaptation, and disaster preparedness.

SMART governance has not helped. SMART leadership has often operated in a vacuum of transparency, pivoting its messaging to suit political convenience and not public accountability, often relying on spin to distract from abysmal performance and losing sight of a fundamental truth: they serve the public, not the other way around.

The SMART commuter train has arrived at the end of the line. After years of unmet promises, low ridership, and growing public frustration, the experiment in regional rail has failed to justify its cost. Continuing to pour tax dollars into a system that so few use is not merely wasteful—it's irresponsible. The time has come to face the music: dismantle the SMART commuter rail agency and remove it from the local taxpayer dole. The era of local taxpayer support for this boondoggle must end.

Notes

1 Timothy Lipman (Consultant financed by NotSoSmart.org.): "Estimated Greenhouse Gas Emission Impacts and Cost-Effectiveness of the Sonoma-Marin SMART Train," February 15, 2020.

2 SMART Annual Report FY 2010 @ 8.

3 Kevin Fixler, "SMART Withholds Daily and Weekly Ridership Records as Train Seats Go Unfilled," *Press Democrat*, December 12, 2019.

4 Editorial Board, "Editorial: SMART Train Tax—IJ Board Recommends No Vote on Measure 1," February 1, 2020, https://www.marinij.com/2020/02/01/editorial-smart-train-tax-ij-recommends-no-vote-on-measure-i/).

5 Fair Political Practices Commission, Complaint Number COM- 01152020-00071.

6 Carruthers, Will. "Marin Country Ballot Measure Campaigns Heat Up. *Pacific Sun*, February 26, 2020.

7 Dan Brekke, "Voters Reject SMART Train Sales Tax Extension in Sonoma and Marin," KQED, March 3, 2020: https://www.kqed.org/news/11804544/smart-train-sales-tax-extension-headed-for-defeat-in-sonoma-and-marin.

8 Will Houston, "SMART, Critics Assess Aftermath of Tax Extension Failure," *Marin Independent Journal,* March 4, 2020.

9 Library of Congress. "Today in History: May 10." https://www.loc.gov/item/today-in-history/may-10/.

10 Wood, Jim. "Remnants of the Rail Era." *Marin Magazine*, July 17, 2022. https://marinmagazine.com/community/history/remnants-of-the-rail-era/.

11 Ibid.

12 Burns, Ryan. "The Disappearing Railroad Blues." *North Coast Journal*, August 18, 2025. https://www.northcoastjournal.com/news/the-disappearing-railroad-blues-2258519.

13 Ibid.

14 "Railroads in California: Map, History, Abandoned Lines." American Rails. Accessed October 6, 2025. https://www.american-rails.com/clfa.html.

15 Wood, Jim. "Remnants of the Rail Era." *Marin Magazin*e, July 17, 2022. https://marinmagazine.com/community/history/remnants-of-the-rail-era/.

16 California Debt Advisory Commission. "State and Local Tax and Bond Ballot Measures: Summary of General Election Results," November 6, 1990.

17 California Special Districts Association, "Proposition 218 Guide for Special Districts," at 6 (general vs. special taxes).

18 California Budget Project, "PROPOSITION 13: ITS IMPACT ON CALIFORNIA AND IMPLICATIONS," April 1997, https://calbudgetcenter.org/app/uploads/2018/09/Issue-Brief_Proposition-13-Its-Impact-on-California-and-Implications_04.1997.pdf.

19 Peter Fimrite, "Commuter Chronicles. 2 Ballot Measures Address North Bay Transportation Woes: Growth, Open Space Also in Package," *SF Gate*, October 19, 1998.

20 Ibid.

21 Ibid.

22 Ibid.

23 https://www.conservationaction.org/

24 Cal Thorpe Associates Consulting Team, "Sonoma Marin Multi Modal-Transportation and Land Use Study," June 6, 1997, at xi.

25 Sonoma-Marin Area Rail Transit District, Assembly Bill No. 224, Chapter 341, Part 16; Chapter 1. General Provisions and Definitions, 105001, at 6–7.

26 California Public Utilities Code § 105104 (emphasis added).

27 https://www.sonomamarintrain.org/about-district

28 "Backers Hope Local Focus Will Help Tax Pass," *Marin Independent Journal,* March 22, 2004.

29 "County Gears Up for New Ballot Measure," *Marin Independent Journal,* March 21, 2004.

30 J. Moore Methods: Public Opinion Research, SMART Survey Results, March 1–8, 2006.

31 SMART 2006 Expenditure Plan, June 21, 2006, at 7.

32 "Backers Say Project Is Viable," Part III, *Marin Independent Journal,* March 23, 2004.

33 "County Gears Up for New Ballot Measure," *Marin Independent Journal*, March 21, 2004; "Backers Say Project Is Viable," *Marin Independent Journal,* March 23, 2004.

34 "Rail Plan Showdown," *Marin Independent Journal,* August 23, 2006.

35 "Taxing Traffic: Marin's Transit Future," *Marin Independent Journal,* March 23, 2004.

36 "County Gears Up for New Ballot Measure," *Marin Independent Journal,* March 21, 2004.

37 Voter Pamphlet for Measure R, 2006.

38 Ibid.

39 Ibid.

40 "County Gears Up for New Ballot Measure," *Marin Independent Journal,* March 21, 2004.

41 Ballot arguments against Measure R.

42 *Marin Independent Journal*, March 21, 2004.

43 https://ballotpedia.org/ (November 2006).

44 Voter Pamphlet, Measure Q, 2008.

45 Ibid.

46 https://ballotpedia.org/ (November 2008)

47 Marin County Civil Grand Jury Report, "SMART: Steep Grade Ahead," June 18, 2010.

48 Ibid. at 1.

49 Ibid. at 8–9.

50 *Marin Independent Journal*, March 21, 2004.

51 Marin County Civil Grand Jury Report. "SMART: Steep Grade Ahead," June 18, 2010, at 7.

52 Ibid. at 15.

53 SMART Board of Director response, dated August 12, 2010 to Grand Jury Report, at 4.

54 Ibid.

55 "SMART General Manager Farhad Mansourian announces he will retire in August," *Press Democrat,* April 21, 2021.

56 White Paper No. 1, February 2008, at 2.

57 White Paper No. 7, July 2008 at 1.

58 *Trains Magazine* archives.

59 Sonoma-Marin Area Transit Project Environmental Impact Report, June 2006, at 3.2:10–11.

60 Sonoma-Marin Area Rail Transit District Annual Report 2017, at 3.

61 The Marin Conversation League Assessment of the Sonoma-Marin Area Rail Transit (SMART) Project, September 8, 2006, at 1.

62 2006 SMART Measure R Mailer.

63 The Marin Conversation League Assessment of the Sonoma-Marin Area Rail Transit (SMART) Project, September 8, 2006, at 1.

64 2006 SMART Expenditure Plan, at 5.

65 Ibid.

66 2006 SMART Expenditure Plan for Measure R, at 6.

67 Ibid. at 1.

68 Ibid. at 7.

69 SMART White Paper No. 18, July 2008.
70 2007 National Transit Data Base, https://www.transit.dot.gov/ntd.
71 2008 SMART Project Funding Plan for Measure Q, at 11.
72 Ibid. at 4.
73 Ibid. at 18.
74 Ibid. at 9.
75 Ibid. at 18.
76 SMART Measure Q: Annual Report to the Public, Fiscal year 2009–2010, at 6.
77 TAM Executive Summary, June 23, 2011, at 4.
78 "TAM Board Doesn't Reconsider SMART Vote," *Patch*, July 8, 2011.
79 TAM's Executive Summary for the July 7, 2011 meeting.
80 Email from Joanne Parker (SMART) to Shruti Hari (MTC) on June 30, 2020.
81 TAM's Executive Summary for the July 7, 2011 meeting.
82 TAM Board Meeting, July 11, 2011.
83 "TAM Board Doesn't Reconsider SMART Vote," *Patch*, July 8, 2011.
84 The Marin Conversation League Assessment of the Sonoma-Marin Area Rail Transit (SMART) Project, September 8, 2006, at 2.
85 Marin County Civil Grand Jury, 2023 Report, at 8.
86 SMART White Paper # 10, May 2008.
87 2019 Marin County Civil Grand Jury Report, at 10.
88 SMART White Paper No. 7, July 2008.
89 SMART White Paper #2, February 2008, at 1.
90 SMART Project Description, "What is SMART," May 2008.
91 SMART White Paper. No. 6, at 1, 3.
92 The Marin Conversation League Assessment of the Sonoma-Marin Area Rail Transit (SMART) Project, September 8, 2006, at 3.
93 MCR Comment Letter on Draft SMART EIR, January 20, 2006.
94 Goldman Sachs, "Electric Vehicles Are Forecast to Be Half of Global Car Sales by 2035," February 10, 2023.

95 Denise-Marie Ordway, "Ballot Measures: Research on How Ballot Format, Wording and News Coverage Affect Voters," *The Journalist's Resource*, September 22, 2023, https://journalistsresource.org/politics-and-government/ballot-measures-election-research/.

96 Kevin Fahey, Carol S. Weissert, and Matthew J. Uttermark, "Extra, Extra, (Don't) Roll-off about It! Newspaper Endorsements for Ballot Measures," *State Politics & Policy Quarterly* 18, no. 1, January 25, 2021, https://doi.org/10.1177/1532440018759269.

97 "Railroaded: Behind the Scenes of SMART's Freight Takeover," Part I, *Bohemian/Pacific Sun*, November 3, 2011.

98 Ibid.

99 Ibid.

100 Ibid.

101 Ibid.

102 https://law.justia.com/codes/california/2022/code-gov/title-2/division-3/part-4-5/chapter-1/section-13978-9/

103 "Railroaded: Behind the Scenes of SMART's Freight Takeover," Part I, *Bohemian/Pacific Sun*, November 3, 2011.

104 Ibid.

105 Ibid.

106 Ibid.

107 Ibid.

108 Carrauthers, Will. "Train Lines: How Two Press Democrat Owners Finessed a Petaluma Real Estate Deal." *Bohemian*. November 20, 2021. https://bohemian.com/train-lines/.

109 "Ethical Journalism." March 26, 2025. *New York Times*. https://www.nytimes.com/editorial-standards/ethical-journalism.html#introductionAndPurpose.

110 "Policies and Standards." *Washington Post*. Updated March 25, 2025; published January 1, 2021. https://www.washingtonpost.com/policies-and-standards/#facts.

111 Society of Professional Journalists. "SPJ Code of Ethics." Revised September 6, 2014. https://www.spj.org/ethicscode.asp.

112 "The Journalism Code of Practice." https://journalism codeofpractice.org/.

113 Standards and practices. *San Francisco Chronicle*. Accessed October 6, 2025. https://www.sfchronicle.com/standards/.

114 "Ethics Policy." *Mercury News*. https://www.mercurynews.com /ethics-policy/.

115 The Editorial Board, "Our Long and Public Record of Supporting Rail," *Press Democrat*, February 20, 2020.

116 Ibid.

117 Ibid.

118 Ibid.

119 Ibid.

120 Ibid.

121 Editorial, "Give Low-Income Riders an Affordable Option on SMART," *Press Democrat,* July 20, 2020.

122 The Editorial Board, "Our Long and Public Record of Supporting Rail," *Press Democrat*, February 20, 2020.

123 "SMART's Immediate Goal Must Be to Reach Ridership Projections," *Marin Independent Journal*, July 22, 2023.

124 Editorial: "Yes on Measure I: Don't Derail the SMART Train," *Press Democrat*, February 2, 2020.

125 "SMART Eyes Freight Storage Options After Drastic Revenue Decline," *Marin Independent Journal*, July 19, 2023.

126 Editorial, "What Was SMART Board Thinking?" *Press Democrat*, August 25, 2011.

127 Editorial, "Even Supreme Court Justices Should Follow Clear Ethics Rules," *Press Democrat*, June 28, 2023.

128 Editorial, "Railroad Square and the Risk of Great Expectations," *Press Democrat*, July 14, 2016.

129 "Sonoma Media Investments, Parent Company of *The Press Democrat,* Sold to One of America's News Giants," *Press Democrat*, May 1, 2025.

130 SMART 2008 Expenditure Plan, at 12.

131 Measure Q (2008).

132 Voter Pamphlet, Measure Q Ballot Argument and Expenditure Plan, at SMM-1.

133 Ibid., at SMM-2.

134 Sonoma County Civil Grand Jury, Final Report 2013–2014, F9.

135 SMART Measure Q Annual Report to the Public, Executive Summary, at 1.

136 2010 Marin County Civil Grand Jury, Recommendation #8, at 15.

137 "SMART urged to put bike path on hold: Marin Grand Jury Criticizes Agency's pension benefits," *Press Democrat*, June 30, 2010.

138 "Cloverdale Line Delayed 3–5 Years," *Press Democrat*, November 3, 2010.

139 "Marin Officials Want New Studies on Viability of SMART," *Press Democrat*, November 29, 2010.

140 "SMART Ready to Finalize Cuts, Approve Bond Sales," *Press Democrat*, April 18, 2011.

141 "SMART Rail Plan Could Face Changes, Delay," *Press Democrat*, July 21, 2011.

142 "Sonoma-Marin Commuter Rail Plan Chugs Along Toward 2016 Start," *Press Democrat*, December 22, 2013.

143 "SMART Confronts Debate over Fares Set for North Bay Rail Service," *Press Democrat*, July 3, 2016.

144 Ibid.

145 "Upfront: Waiting on a Train, Ever Get the Feeling That SMART Was a Dumb Idea After All?" *Pacific Sun*, March 16, 2017.

146 Ibid.

147 "North Bay's SMART Commuter Rail System to Roll After Long Delays," *San Francisco Chronicle*, July 30, 2017.

148 "SMART Announces Start of Full Service Aug. 25," *Press Democrat*, August 17, 2017.

149 "Taking Stock of the SMART Train on Its Anniversary," *Marin Independent Journal*, August 15, 2018.

150 SMART White Paper # 1, February 2008.

151 Corey, Canapary & Galanis Research and Counsel in Marketing, SMART Onboard survey, Summary Report, Spring 2018, at 16-18.

152 Jacobs Carter Burgess, Inc. in Association with Parsons Brinckerhoff, Inc. and KNN Public Finance, SMART Project Funding Plan, July 2008, at 5.

153 "Round Trips," *Press Democrat*, March 6, 2011.

154 "Fares for California's SMART Commuter Trains Questioned," *Press Democrat*, July 5, 2016.

155 "SMART Announces Start of Full Service Aug. 25," *Press Democrat*, August 17, 2017.

156 Ibid.

157 SMART Ridership for Web Posting.xlsx.

158 https://www.whitehouse.gov/briefing-room/statements-releases/2021/09/13/president-biden-announces-10-key-nominations-2/

159 Public Policy Institute of California, "Making the Most of Transit: Density, Employment Growth, and Ridership around New Stations," February 2011, at 2.

160 "Eliminating Public Transit's First-Mile/Last-Mile Problem," *Human Transit*, July 2020.

161 "TAM response to Grand Jury Report on Smart first mile." Accessed October 6, 2025. https://www.tam.ca.gov/wp-content/uploads/2019/06/11b-TAM-Resp-to-Grand-Jury-Rpt-SMART-First-Last-Mile.pdf.

162 "Smart Launches on Demand Microtransit Shuttle Connecting the Train to the Sonoma County Airport (STS)." County Of Sonoma. Accessed October 6, 2025. https://sonomacounty.ca.gov/smart-launches-on-demand-microtransit-shuttle-connecting-the-train-to-the-sonoma-county-airport-(sts).

163 Ibid.

164 “Making the Most of Transit: Density, Employment Growth, and Ridership around New Stations,” Public Policy Institute of California, February 2011, at 14.

165 “Ridership Reports.” Sonoma, August 18, 2025. https://www.sonomamarintrain.org/RidershipReports.

166 Sonoma-Marin Area Rail Transit (SMART) ridership. Accessed October 6, 2025. https://sonomamarintrain.org/sites/default/files/Documents/SMART%20Ridership%20Web%20Posting_1.24.pdf.

167 “SMART withholds daily and weekly ridership records as train seats go unfilled,” *Press Democrat*, December 12, 2019.

168 “SMART Ridership Declined in 2nd Year, but Weekday Use Growing, Newly Obtained Records Show,” *Press Democrat*, January 3, 2020.

169 Ibid.

170 California, State of. “Traffic Operations.” Traffic Operations | Caltrans. Accessed October 6, 2025. https://dot.ca.gov/programs/traffic-operations.

171 Sonoma-Marin Area Rail Transit Project: Final Environmental Impact Report, June 2006, at 3.2-11.

172 “Arguments For Measure R” and “Rebuttal to Arguments Against,” Sonoma-Marin Area Rail Transit District Measure R, 2006.

173 Sonoma-Marin Area Rail Transit District Measure Q Mailer.

174 *Press Democrat*, May 19, 2020.

175 *Press Democrat*, January 14, 2022.

176 Ibid.

177 Ibid.

178 *Press Democrat*, January 19, 2022.

179 Final Report Freight Market Analysis, December 9, 2021, at 24-28.

180 Ibid.

181 Ibid.

182 Ibid.

183 *Press Democrat*, January 14, 2022.

184 Bernard Meyers, "The NCRA Boondoggle: From Bankruptcy to Bankruptcy in 30 years," November 9, 2021.

185 Final Report Freight Market Analysis, December 9, 2021, at 26.

186 Ibid.

187 Ibid.

188 SMART Board of Directors Meeting Agenda, December 2022, at 19-20.

189 SMART Board of Directors Meeting Agenda, December 2023, at 26-27.

190 *Marin Independent Journal,* July 2023.

191 "Shipping by Rail vs Truck: Everything You Need to Know," *Truckload Shipping*, October 23, 2023; "Freight Shipping by Train vs. Truck: Advantages and Disadvantages," *Freightera, Freight Marketplace*, June 2023; "Train vs. Truck: Which is Better for Freight Shipping," *Seminole Gulf Railway.*

192 SMART Board of Directors Meeting Agenda, December 2023, at 15.

193 "SMART Eyes Freight Storage Options After Drastic Revenue Decline," *Marin Independent Journal*, July 23, 2021.

194 *Marin Independent Journal,* November 16, 2023.

195 *Marin Independent Journal,* July 19, 2023.

196 "SMART Leans Toward Gas Tanker Storage to Regain Revenue," *Marin Independent Journal*, November 16, 2023.

197 *Marin Independent Journal,* July 19, 2023.

198 SMART Board of Directors Meeting Agenda, December 2023, at 14.

199 SMART Board of Directors Meeting Agenda, December 2023, at 15.

200 SMART Board of Directors Meeting, November 15, 2023, Public Comments, at 3.

201 Ibid.

202 Ibid.

203 *Marin Independent Journal,* November 16, 2023.

204 Michael Kruse, "The Escalator Ride That Changed America," *Politico*, June 14, 2019.

205 *Christian Monitor*, June 18, 2015; *Hollywood Reporter*, June 17, 2015.

206 Ibid.

207 Robert Longley, "What Is Astroturfing in Politics?" *Thought Co.*, October 14, 2020.

208 SMART AT A CROSSROADS: HERE TODAY, GONE TOMORROW? 2022–2023 Marin County Civil Grand Jury, June 22, 2023.

209 Ibid. 1, 9.

210 SMART at a Crossroads, Here Today, Gone Tomorrow, Marin County Civil Grand Jury, June 22, 2023, at 1-16.

211 *Marin Independent Journal*, December 22, 2023.

212 *Marin Independent Journal*, September 24, 2023.

213 SMART Board of Director Agenda, December 2023 at 33.

214 *Press Democrat*, October 11, 2023.

215 https://www.factcheck.org/2017/01/the-facts-on-crowd-size/

216 SMART Board Packet, December 20, 2023, at 7.

217 SMART Expenditure Plan, July 2006 at 5.

218 SMART Expenditure Plan, July 2008 at 13.

219 SMART Expenditure Plan, 2019.

220 SMART Board Packet, May 17, 2023, at 136.

221 *Marin Independent Journal*, November 23, 2023.

222 Memorandum from Mike Arnold to the SMART Board, dated January 15, 2024.

223 SMART AT A CROSSROADS HERE TODAY, GONE TOMORROW? 2022–2023 Marin County Civil Grand Jury, June 22, 2023.

224 SMART Board Packet, December 20, 2023, at 7-9.

225 SMART Board Packet, December 20, 2023, at 7-9 & 182.

226 *Marin Independent Journal*, December 22, 2023.

227 Ibid.

228 National Transit Database, National Summaries and Trends, Federal Transit Administration, U.S. Department of Transportation (2020) at 20–21. See also: https://www.transitwiki.org/TransitWiki/index.php/Farebox_Recovery_Ratio#:~:text=The%20figure%20is%20calculated%20by, fare%20structure%2C%20and%20ridership%20patterns

229 Statistical Summary of Bay Area Transit Operators (July 2015) at 3–6.

230 National Transit Database, October 2023 Comparable Monthly Ridership excel spreadsheet (cost per miles is column Y divided by column X and cost per rider is column Y divided column V).

231 Assembly Bill 2224, Chapter 9 (Dissolution).

232 SMART AT A CROSSROADS HERE TODAY, GONE TOMORROW? 2022–2023 Marin County Civil Grand Jury, June 22, 2023, at 13.

233 Kim Parker, Juliana Menasce Horowitz, and Rachel Minkin, "How the Coronavirus Outbreak Has – and Hasn't – Changed the Way Americans Work," Pew Research Center, December 9, 2020.

234 Katherine Haan and Kelly Main, "Remote Work Statistics and Trends in 2024," *Forbes Advisor,* July 2023.

235 Skylar Woodhouse, "U.S. Public Transit Faces Funding Crisis Amid Remote Work," Government Technology (Transportation), *Bloomberg News*, May 10, 2023.

236 Ibid.

237 Robert Spotswood, *Marin Independent Journal*, May 2, 2023.

238 Tanya Snyder, Shia Kapos, Lisa Kasinsky, and Wes Venteicher, "Remote work Is Straining Public Transit," *Politico*, May 2023.

239 Steve Greenhut, "Transit Bailout Will Only Delay the Day of Reckoning," Pacific Research Institute, June 29, 2023.

240 Brian Taylor and Jacob Wasserman, "For the Press: Transportation, and Covid-19," UCLA Institute of Transportation Studies, September 8, 2022.

241 Abubakr Ziedan, Candace Brakewood, Kari Watkins, "Will transit recover? A retrospective study of nationwide ridership in the United States during the COVID-19 pandemic," National Library of Medicine, June 24, 2023.

242 Ibid.

243 SMART Board Packet, December 20, 2023, at 70.

244 SMART Board Packet, December 7, 2022, at 64.

245 SMART Board Packet, December 20, 2023, at 33.

246 Tanya Snyder, Shia Kapos, Lisa Kasinsky, and Wes Venteicher, "Remote Work Is Straining Public Transit," *Politico*, May 2023.

247 Peer Coy, "Working from Home Is Here to Stay (and for Good Reason)," *New York Times,* April 10, 2023.

248 Sarah Kessler, "Remote Work May Be Stickier than You Think," *New York Times DealBook,* January 2023.

249 Bay Area Council Employer Network: Return to Work Office Tracking Poll.

250 Adriana Rezal, "The New Normal Is Hybrid: How S.F. Compares with Other Cities in Offering Remote Work," *San Francisco Chronicle*, March 2023.

251 Skip Descant, "Remote Work Flipped the Commuting Script. Now Transit Must Adapt," *Government Technology (Transportation)*, December 2022.

252 Grace Mayer, "CEO says there's a false assumption that people like commuting into a business hub: 'They don't. It's a complete waste of time and money,'" *Business Insider,* March 8, 2023.

253 Joel Rose, "Public transit systems try to avoid a 'death spiral' as remote work hurts ridership," NPR, November 15, 2023.

254 Tanya Snyder, Shia Kapos, Lisa Kasinsky, and Wes Venteicher, "Remote Work Is Straining Public Transit," *Politico*, May 2023.

255 Because SMART continues to suppress how many of its riders don't pay, these numbers represent a rough estimate by calculating the increase in ridership since SMART allowed youth and seniors to ride for free.

256 Spending estimates are drawn from BLS Consumer Expenditure Survey patterns, scaled to California cost of living.

257 Chapter 9 (Dissolution) of Assembly Bill 2224.

258 California Public Utilities Code § 105330.

259 Assembly Bill No. 2224, Chapter 34, Sec. 4. Part 16, SONOMA-MARIN AREA RAIL TRANSIT DISTRICT. Chapter 9. Dissolution (California Public Utilities Code).

260 Ibid., §§ 105333-34; 105337.

261 Ibid., § 105336.

262 "SMART at a Crossroads Here Today, Gone Tomorrow," 2022–2023 Marin County Civil Grand Jury, June 22, 2023.

263 Ibid., 8.

264 SMART Board Meeting September 20, 2023.

265 Ibid.

266 Ibid.

267 Ibid.

268 Ibid.

269 Ibid.

270 Ibid. and Memorandum dated September 20, 2023 from Heather McKillop, Chief Financial Officer, to SMART Board of Directors.

271 Tom Vacar, "Is the Marin Sonoma SMART Train Doomed?" KTVU FOX 2, September 25, 2023.

272 SMART Board Meeting, September 20, 2023.

273 "SMART Builds Its Case for Tax Renewal" *Press Democrat*, October 8, 2023.

274 "SMART Plans Communications Campaign in Response to Grand Jury Report," *Marin Independent Journal*, October 21, 2023.

275 Ibid.

276 Memorandum dated November 13, 2023, to Transportation Authority of Marin (TAM), Funding, Programs & Legislation Executive Committee, from Anne Richman, TAM Executive Director and David Chan, TAM Director of Programming and Legislation.

277 Ibid.

278 "Would Sonoma County Voters Approve a Climate Tax?" *Argus Courier*, April 23, 2023.

279 Marin Voice: "Are Marin Voters Running out of Generosity Toward Tax Revenues?" *Marin Independent Journal*, May 25, 2017.

280 https://ballotpedia.org/Sales_tax_in_California#2023.

281 Ibid.

282 Marin Voice: "Are Marin Voters Running out of Generosity Toward Tax Revenues?" *Marin Independent Journal*, May 25, 2017.

283 John Woolfolk, "Bay Area poll finds tepid support for public transit—a far cry from the days when voters eagerly threw money at it," *Bay Area News Group*, October 3, 2023.

284 Dick Spotswood, "No Surprise to See Bay Area Taxpayers' Patience Wearing Thin," *Marin Independent Journal*, October 17, 2023.

285 Ibid.

286 Marin Voice: "We Need to Protect Homeowners as Property Tax Proposals Pile Up," *Marin Independent Journal*, February 17, 2024.

287 Deborah Block, "Free Public Transportation Accelerates in Some US Cities" *VOA News*, February 23, 2023.

288 Legislative Analyst's office. "California's Cap and Trade Program." Accessed October 6, 2025. https://lao.ca.gov/Publications/Report/4811.

289 Metropolitan Transportation Commission. "Cap and Trade Funding." https://mtc.ca.gov/funding/state-funding/cap-and-trade-funding.